Date: 12/17/14

How to Use This Book

Look for these special features in this book:

SIDEBARS, **CHARTS**, **GRAPHS**, and original **MAPS** expand your understanding of what's being discussed—and also make useful sources for classroom reports.

FAQs answer common **F**requently **A**sked **Q**uestions about people, places, and things.

WOW FACTORS offer "Who knew?" facts to keep you thinking.

TRAVEL GUIDE gives you tips on exploring the state—either in person or right from your chair!

PROJECT ROOM provides fun ideas for school assignments and incredible research projects. Plus, there's a guide to primary sources—what they are and how to cite them.

Please note: All statistics are as up-to-date as possible at the time of publication.
Population data is taken from the 2010 census.

Consultants: Katherine R. Bruner, Department of Geology and Geography,
West Virginia University; Carletta A. Bush, Department of History, West Virginia University;
William Loren Katz

Book production by The Design Lab

Library of Congress Cataloging-in-Publication Data
Heinrichs, Ann.
 West Virginia / by Ann Heinrichs. — Revised edition.
    pages cm. — (America the beautiful, third series)
 Includes bibliographical references and index.
 Audience: Ages 9–12.
 ISBN 978-0-531-28299-1 (library binding : alk. paper)
 1. West Virginia—Juvenile literature. I. Title.
 F241.3.H453 2014
 975.4—dc23   2013046231

1 2 3 4 5 6 7 8 9 10 R 24 23 22 21 20 19 18 17 16 15

AMERICA ★ THE ★ BEAUTIFUL

West Virginia

BY ANN HEINRICHS

Third Series, Revised Edition

Children's Press®
An Imprint of Scholastic Inc.
New York ★ Toronto ★ London ★ Auckland ★ Sydney
Mexico City ★ New Delhi ★ Hong Kong
Danbury, Connecticut

CONTENTS

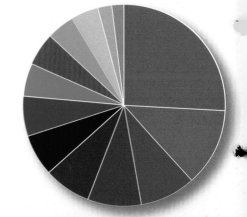

4 GROWTH AND CHANGE

The issue of slavery tears the nation apart, and it tears Virginia apart, too. But the independent-minded western Virginians create a new state for themselves. **40**

MORE MODERN TIMES

5

West Virginians deal with coalfield wars, unemployment, civil rights, mine safety, and environmental protection. **54**

9 TRAVEL GUIDE

Ride the rapids, tour a mine, explore a cave, ride a steam train through the mountains, or visit a history museum. Whatever you enjoy, you'll find it in West Virginia! **104**

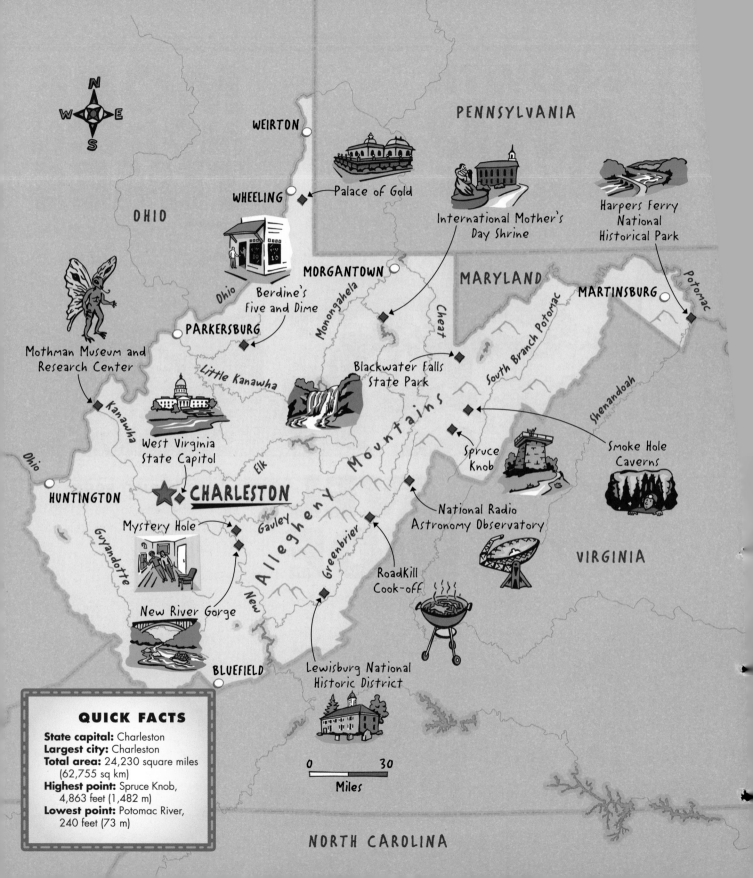

PENNSYLVANIA

WEIRTON

Palace of Gold

International Mother's
Day Shrine

Harpers Ferry
National
Historical Park

WHEELING

OHIO

MORGANTOWN

MARYLAND

MARTINSBURG

Potomac

Berdine's
Five and Dime

Ohio

Monongahela

Cheat

South Branch Potomac

PARKERSBURG

Mothman Museum and
Research Center

Little Kanawha

Blackwater Falls
State Park

Shenandoah

West Virginia
State Capitol

Kanawha

Elk

Allegheny Mountains

Spruce
Knob

Smoke Hole
Caverns

Ohio

CHARLESTON

Mystery Hole

Gauley

National Radio
Astronomy Observatory

HUNTINGTON

VIRGINIA

Guyandotte

New

Greenbrier

RoadKill
Cook-off

New River Gorge

BLUEFIELD

Lewisburg National
Historic District

NORTH CAROLINA

0   30
Miles

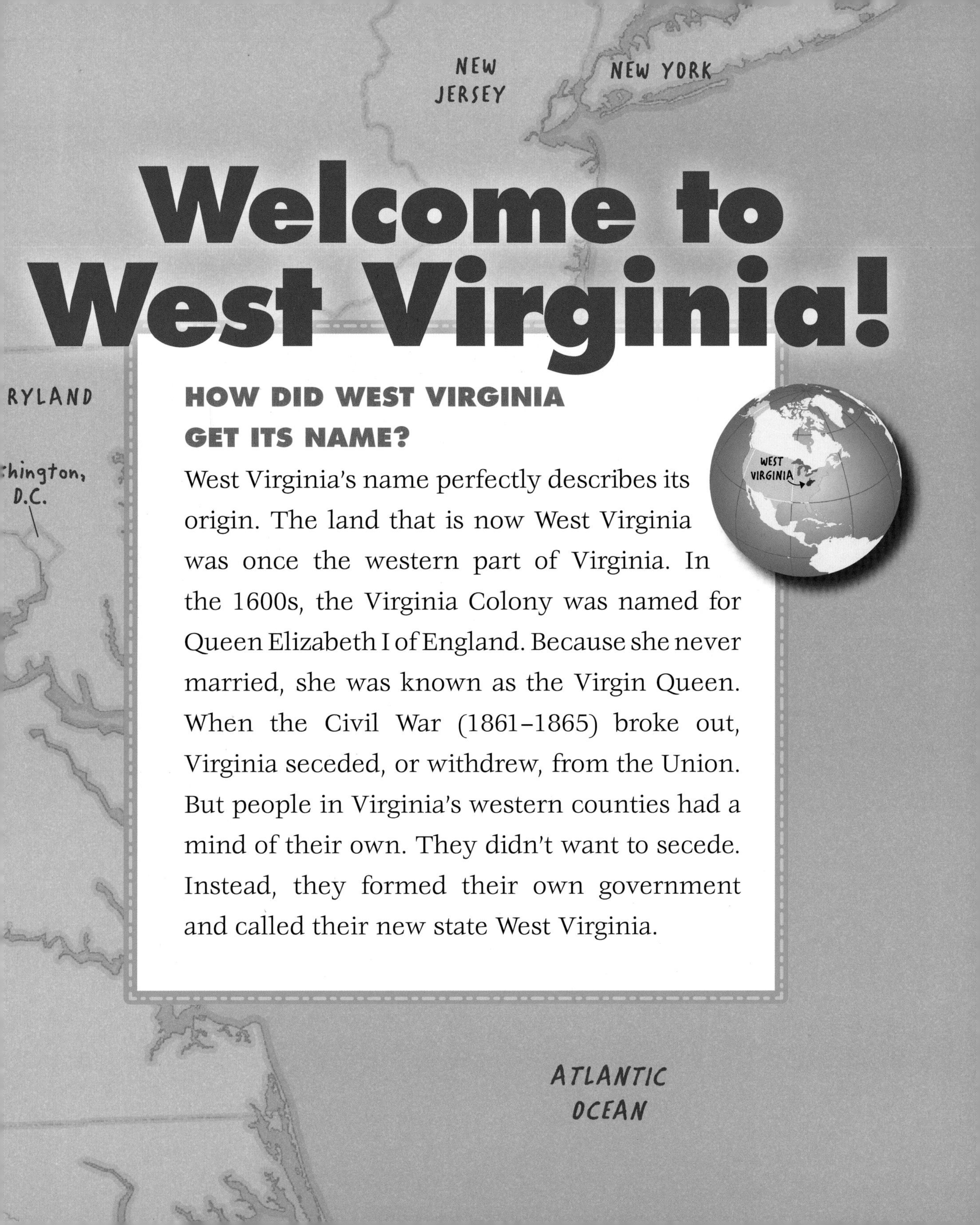

Welcome to West Virginia!

HOW DID WEST VIRGINIA GET ITS NAME?

West Virginia's name perfectly describes its origin. The land that is now West Virginia was once the western part of Virginia. In the 1600s, the Virginia Colony was named for Queen Elizabeth I of England. Because she never married, she was known as the Virgin Queen. When the Civil War (1861–1865) broke out, Virginia seceded, or withdrew, from the Union. But people in Virginia's western counties had a mind of their own. They didn't want to secede. Instead, they formed their own government and called their new state West Virginia.

WEST
VIRGINIA

RYLAND

chington,
D.C.

ATLANTIC
OCEAN

READ ABOUT

The New River winds
through Hawks
Nest State Park.

CHAPTER ONE

LAND

★

WEST VIRGINIA IS THE ONLY STATE THAT LIES COMPLETELY WITHIN A MOUNTAIN RANGE. All of its 24,230 square miles (62,755 square kilometers) are nestled in the Appalachian Mountains. Of all the states east of the Mississippi River, West Virginia has the highest average elevation. Even the state's lowest point, along the Potomac River near Harpers Ferry, is 240 feet (73 meters) above sea level. Its tallest peak, Spruce Knob, rises 4,863 feet (1,482 m) high.

West Virginia Topography

Use the color-coded elevation chart to see on the map West Virginia's high points (dark red to orange) and low points (green to dark green). Elevation is measured as the distance above or below sea level.

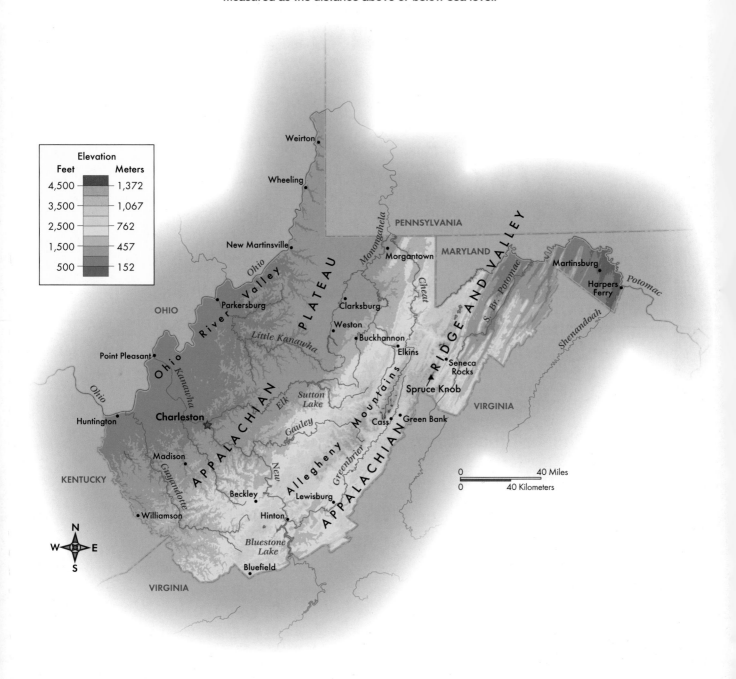

Elevation

Feet		Meters
4,500		1,372
3,500		1,067
2,500		762
1,500		457
500		152

THE PANHANDLE STATE

If you look at a map of West Virginia, you might think it's shaped like a frog with two long rear legs. West Virginians see those "legs" as two long handles of a pan. They're known as the Northern **Panhandle** and the Eastern Panhandle. That's why West Virginia is sometimes called the Panhandle State.

West Virginia is sandwiched between the northeastern states and the southern states. Because of its in-between position, geographers include it in many different regions. The U.S. Census Bureau classifies West Virginia as a southern state.

Most of West Virginia's borders are jagged because they're outlined by mountains and rivers. The state is bordered by Pennsylvania to the north, Ohio to the north-

Windblown trees on Spruce Knob in Monongahela National Forest

WORD TO KNOW

panhandle *a narrow strip of land that juts out from a broader area*

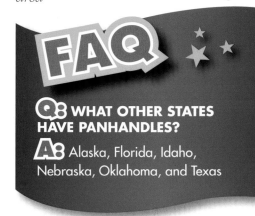

FAQ

Q8 WHAT OTHER STATES HAVE PANHANDLES?

A8 Alaska, Florida, Idaho, Nebraska, Oklahoma, and Texas

west, Kentucky to the southwest, Virginia to the south and east, and Maryland to the east and north. The Potomac River and its North Branch flow along the northern edge of the Eastern Panhandle to form part of West Virginia's border with Maryland. The Ohio River, West Virginia's largest river, forms the state's western border with Ohio. A **tributary** of the Ohio River, the Big Sandy River, forms part of the border with Kentucky.

Rivers functioned as highways in the state's early days, and riverside towns became West Virginia's biggest cities. Charleston, the state capital and largest city, grew up along the Kanawha River. Wheeling, Parkersburg, and Huntington are major cities along the Ohio River. Morgantown and Fairmont lie along the Monongahela River.

WORD TO KNOW

tributary *a river that flows into a larger river*

West Virginia Geo-Facts

Along with the state's geographical highlights, this chart ranks West Virginia's land, water, and total area compared to all other states.

Total area; rank . . . . . . 24,230 square miles (62,755 sq km); 41st
Land; rank . . . . 24,038 square miles (62,258 sq km); 41st
Water; rank . . . . 192 square miles (497 sq km); 50th
Inland water; rank . . . . 192 square miles (497 sq km); 46th
Geographic center . . . . Braxton, 4 miles (6 km) east of Sutton
Latitude . . . . 37°10' N to 40°40' N
Longitude . . . . 77°40' W to 82°40' W
Highest point . . . . Spruce Knob, 4,863 feet (1,482 m)
Lowest point . . . . Potomac River, 240 feet (73 m)
Largest city . . . . Charleston
Longest river . . . . Ohio River

Source: U.S. Census Bureau, 2010 census

West Virginia would fit inside Alaska, the largest state, 27 times.

The Wheeling Suspension Bridge spans the Ohio River in the town of Wheeling.

LAND REGIONS

West Virginia is a small part of the Appalachian mountain system, a vast chain of mountains that extends all the way from Canada in the north to Alabama in the south. Eastern West Virginia falls within the Appalachian Ridge and Valley region, and western West Virginia lies in the Appalachian **Plateau**.

The Appalachian Ridge and Valley

If you flew over the Appalachian Ridge and Valley region in an airplane, you would see long ridges, or continuous mountains, with long, narrow valleys in between them. This mountain-and-valley system runs in a northeast–southwest line. It was formed about 250 million years ago, as the giant tectonic plates holding Europe, Africa, and

WORD TO KNOW

plateau *a flat, elevated part of the earth with steep slopes*

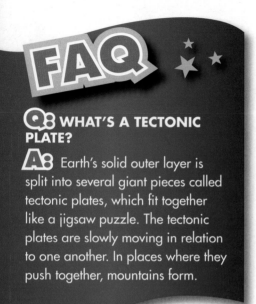

WORD TO KNOW

continental divide *an area of raised terrain that forms a border between two watersheds on a continent*

North America slowly smashed into each other. Running through the Eastern Panhandle is the wide, fertile, and scenic Shenandoah Valley, which falls into this region.

West Virginia's highest mountains are the Allegheny Mountains, in the eastern half of the state. The western edge of the Ridge and Valley region is the Allegheny Front. This is an abrupt rise in elevation, separating the lower Alleghenies to the east from the higher Alleghenies to the west. The Allegheny Front is part of the country's eastern **continental divide**. Waters east of the front flow toward the Atlantic Ocean, while waters to the west eventually enter the Gulf of Mexico. Among the rugged peaks of the Allegheny Front is Spruce Knob. It's the highest point in West Virginia and in the whole Allegheny Mountain range.

The Appalachian Plateau

The Appalachian Plateau covers all the rest of West Virginia, making up more than two-thirds of the state's land area. It's sometimes called the Allegheny Plateau. This is a rugged region, with steep-sloped hillsides, flat-topped mountains, and narrow valleys. This land was thrust upward even higher as the ancient continents ground together. Over millions of years, rivers and streams carved out the plateau's mountains, hills, and valleys. Some of the state's highest mountains rise in the Alleghenies in the eastern part of this region.

The Appalachian Plateau has rich deposits of coal, salt, natural gas, and petroleum. Coal, found in 43 of West Virginia's 55 counties, is the state's most valuable natural resource. Like petroleum and natural gas, it is a fossil fuel. That is, it's made from material that was once living. Coal was formed from trees, ferns, and other plants that lived millions of years ago. Over time, the pressure of soil and rocks turned the material into coal.

Snowfall along the Highland Scenic Highway

CLIMATE

Summers in West Virginia are warm and humid, and July is the hottest month of the year. The valleys are much warmer than the mountains, because temperatures are cooler at higher elevations and the wind cannot easily reach into valleys. In summertime, temperatures in the mountains might be 10°F (6°C) cooler than in the valleys.

Winters in West Virginia are chilly, and the higher mountain areas can get extremely cold. January is the coldest month, however, temperatures vary widely by region. At Spruce Knob, on the Allegheny Front, low temperatures in January average about 16°F (–9°C). At Williamson, near the Kentucky border, the average January low is only about 25°F (–4°C). Lewisburg set the record for West Virginia's lowest temperature. It plunged down to –37°F (–38°C) on December 30, 1917.

THE FLOOD OF 1985

When warm air from the south meets the cool air of high-speed winds from the west, rain and snow can wreak havoc on West Virginia. In 1985, Hurricane Juan ravaged the southern coasts before whirling up to West Virginia. For several days, rain poured down on the Allegheny Mountains, completely soaking the ground. When another storm front dumped 8 inches (20 centimeters) of rain within 24 hours, massive flooding wiped out entire communities.

Q: **WHY IS THE EASTERN PANHANDLE SO DRY?**

A: It's in the rain shadow of the Allegheny Front. A rain shadow is a dry area on the side of a mountain that faces away from the wind. Moist winds from the west bump into the Allegheny Front and deposit rain on its west side. When the wind reaches the east side of the front, the air has lost its moisture. Cactuses are common on the Allegheny's east-facing slopes!

WORD TO KNOW

precipitation *all water that falls to the earth, including rain, sleet, hail, snow, dew, fog, or mist*

West Virginians get plenty of rainfall. On average, the state gets about 44 inches (112 cm) of **precipitation** in the form of rain, snow, and other moisture every year. Like the temperatures, precipitation varies by region. The Eastern Panhandle gets the least precipitation, about 35 inches (89 cm) every year. But mountainous areas get more than 60 inches (152 cm). In the summer, people in the valleys are often drenched by thunderstorms. In the winter, as much as 100 inches (254 cm) of snow may fall in the northern mountains. But the southwestern part of the state gets less than 20 inches (51 cm) of snow a year. When winter snows melt, the water often floods the valleys.

PLANT LIFE

Vast forests once covered West Virginia. Although loggers and settlers have cut down thousands of trees, much forestland still remains. Some of it represents regrowth after heavy cutting in the early 1900s. Today, about 78 percent of West Virginia is covered with forests. Only Maine and New Hampshire have a higher percentage

Weather Report

This chart shows record temperatures (high and low) for the state, as well as average temperatures (July and January) and average annual precipitation for West Virginia.

Record high temperature . . . . 112°F (44°C) at Martinsburg on July 10, 1936
Record low temperature . . . . –37°F (–38°C) at Lewisburg on December 30, 1917
Average July temperature, Charleston . . . . 75°F (24°C)
Average January temperature, Charleston . . . . . . .34°F (1°C)
Average yearly precipitation, Charleston . . .44 inches (112 cm)

Source: National Climatic Data Center, NESDIS, NOAA, U.S. Department of Commerce

West Virginia is home to insect-eating plant species such as the purple pitcher plant.

of forest cover. Some of the state's major forest trees are spruce, pine, hickory, oak, and sugar maple, the state tree. Rhododendron and mountain laurel, both evergreen shrubs, dot hillsides throughout the state. Rhododendron blossoms, in pink and white, are the state flower.

Monongahela National Forest stretches down the eastern part of the state. It encompasses much of the Ridge and Valley region, including the rugged Allegheny Front. Parts of George Washington and Jefferson national forests reach across the eastern border from Virginia. West Virginia also has nine state forests.

High in the Alleghenies are several highland bogs, or wetlands. There you'll find wild blueberries, cranberries, skunk cabbage, and carnivorous (insect-eating) plants such as purple pitcher plants and sundews. Cactus and other dry-weather plants grow on the drier eastern slopes of the Allegheny Front.

SEE IT HERE!

MONONGAHELA NATIONAL FOREST

Monongahela National Forest protects more than 919,000 acres (372,000 hectares) of mountainous forestland. Most of the state's highest peaks are there, including Spruce Knob, the highest of them all. About 75 species of trees grow in the forest, including red spruce, balsam fir, and mountain ash. Six major rivers have their beginnings in Monongahela National Forest: the Monongahela, Potomac, Greenbrier, Elk, Tygart, and Gauley. The Spruce Knob–Seneca Rocks National Recreation Area is located in the forest, too. Visitors to Monongahela National Forest enjoy outdoor activities such as hiking, camping, mountain biking, boating, white-water rafting, cross-country skiing, and bird-watching.

ANIMAL LIFE

With densely forested mountains and valleys, West Virginia provides a sheltered home for a variety of woodland animals. White-tailed deer and black bears roam high in the mountains. Scurrying in the underbrush are smaller animals such as chipmunks, raccoons, skunks, opossums, squirrels, rabbits, bobcats, red and gray foxes, and groundhogs. Beavers and otters are found near the waterways, and trout, bass, pike, and muskellunge glisten in the cool mountain streams.

Waterbirds such as herons and bitterns spend the spring and summer in West Virginia. Loons, ducks, and geese pass through on their annual migrations.

Some black bears make their home in West Virginia's mountains.

West Virginia National Park Areas

This map shows some of West Virginia's national parks, monuments, preserves, and other areas protected by the National Park Service.

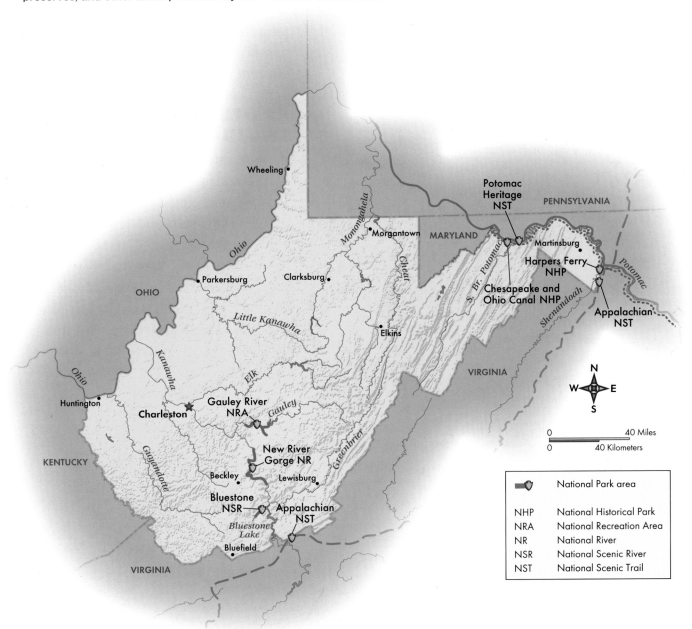

Wheeling

Morgantown

MARYLAND

PENNSYLVANIA

Potomac Heritage NST

Martinsburg

Harpers Ferry NHP

Chesapeake and Ohio Canal NHP

Appalachian NST

Clarksburg

OHIO

Parkersburg

Elkins

VIRGINIA

Little Kanawha

Huntington

KENTUCKY

Charleston

Gauley River NRA

New River Gorge NR

Beckley

Lewisburg

Bluestone NSR

Bluestone Lake

Appalachian NST

Bluefield

VIRGINIA

Ohio

Monongahela

Cheat

S. Br. Potomac

Shenandoah

Potomac

Kanawha

Elk

Gauley

Greenbrier

Guyandotte

N	W E S

0	40 Miles
0	40 Kilometers

	National Park area
NHP	National Historical Park
NRA	National Recreation Area
NR	National River
NSR	National Scenic River
NST	National Scenic Trail

MINI-BIO

MAURICE BROOKS: APPALACHIAN NATURE LOVER

Maurice Brooks (1900–1993) grew up on his family's farm in French Creek. He and his father kept a close eye on the area's birds and their nest-building habits. Later, Brooks became one of the foremost experts on birds and other wildlife of Appalachia. As a professor of forestry and biology at West Virginia University, he inspired his students with the love of Appalachian wildlife. He kept a home at French Creek for much of his life, and today there is a wildlife center in the town.

? Want to know more? Visit www.factsfor now.scholastic.com and enter the keywords **West Virginia**.

Wild turkeys and quail forage for food on the ground, while cardinals, warblers, thrushes, and scarlet tanagers chirp and sing in the trees. Look even higher, and you'll see hawks, eagles, and vultures soaring in the sky. They can soar for hours on the warm air currents rising from the valleys.

PROTECTING THE ENVIRONMENT

West Virginians have a long history of protecting their natural resources. Vast areas of forest trees had been cut in the late 1800s and early 1900s. In 1915, the first parcel of what would be Monongahela National Forest was set aside. Workers planted thousands of new trees there. Today, most of the forest is second-growth forest—that is, trees that have grown back after the original trees were cut down for timber.

ENDANGERED ANIMALS

More than a dozen West Virginia animals are endangered species. That means they're in danger of becoming extinct, or disappearing altogether. One is the eastern cougar, or mountain lion. It once lived throughout West Virginia, but it could be extinct in the state by now. Virginia big-eared bats are another endangered species. They live mainly in the northeast, roosting in a handful of caves. Wildlife protection workers have erected "bat gates" on some of these caves to keep people from harming the bats or scaring them away.

Eastern cougar

An organization called the Nature Conservancy protects more than a dozen sites in West Virginia. One is Bear Rocks Preserve near Petersburg. It's noted for its cranberry bogs and undersized red spruce trees, which have been stunted by wind and cold weather. Another is the Pine Knob Preserve near Franklin. Its oak trees, which have never been cut, are more than 300 years old. Rare plants grow in pockets that preserve ice-age conditions at Ice Mountain.

The West Virginia Department of Environmental Protection monitors the state's land, air, and water. Its workers study mining methods, waste disposal, and many other human activities that put pressure on the environment. Through constant inspections, reports, and regulations, the department makes sure that the state's natural resources stay clean and healthy. On the community level, more and more people are adopting citywide programs to recycle household wastes. They realize that a clean environment starts at home.

A hiker in the Dolly Sods Wilderness Area, one of the many natural places that West Virginia works to preserve

READ ABOUT

Thousands of years
ago, hunters used
stones and spears
to kill large game.

c. 10,500 BCE
*People first enter what is
now West Virginia*

▲ c. 7000 BCE
*Large game animals die
out, and people adapt by
hunting smaller game*

c. 1000 BCE
*People begin settling
in small villages and
building burial mounds*

CHAPTER TWO

FIRST PEOPLE

★

AROUND 12,500 YEARS AGO, THE LAST ICE AGE WAS ENDING AND NORTH AMERICA WAS VERY COLD. Small family groups roamed from place to place following mammoths and other huge animals that provided them with meat to eat and hides to wear. They hunted using spears with chipped-stone points. Groups of people first entered the Ohio and Kanawha river valleys around this time.

c. 250–150 BCE
Adena people build Grave Creek burial mound

c. 1000 CE
People of the Fort Ancient culture begin building large towns in what is now western West Virginia

◄ **c. 1650**
People of the Iroquois Confederacy drive other Native groups out of West Virginia

HUNTERS AND GATHERERS

By about 7000 BCE, the climate warmed, and West Virginia's plants and animals became much like they are today. As large game animals died out, people adapted by hunting deer, bears, rabbits, wild turkeys, and fish. To hunt smaller animals, they invented new weapons, atlatls—or spear-throwers—which gave their spears extra force and speed.

They also gathered nuts, berries, seeds, roots, and other edible plants in the forests. People who lived along the Ohio River in what is now the Northern Panhandle of West Virginia collected freshwater clams to eat. Around 2000 BCE, people began carving stone bowls for preparing food. Eventually, they began growing food plants such as sunflowers.

MOUND BUILDERS

Around 1000 BCE, people began to organize themselves into settled villages. They grew more and more of their own food on small farm plots. People built circular homes with wooden poles for walls. They covered their roofs

SEE IT HERE!

DELF NORONA MUSEUM

What was life like for the Adena people? You'll find out at the Delf Norona Museum in Moundsville. It's right next to Grave Creek Mound. Exhibits display objects found in the mound, such as jewelry, pottery, arrowheads, tools, shells, and beads. You'll learn about the Adena people's cultural life and daily activities and how they likely built their massive burial mound.

It took a tremendous amount of labor to build Grave Creek Mound. The builders hauled about 60,000 tons of dirt to the site, one basketful at a time!

Picture Yourself . . .

in an Adena Village

As you wake up in the morning, you gaze up toward the high, pointed ceiling. Smoke from the morning fire is already streaming upward. Around the spacious hut, your parents, sisters, and grandparents are preparing for the day ahead.

Glancing through the wall of woven branches, you see your family's garden of sunflowers and squash. Soon it will be time for the harvest festival. Then, in the fall, your father will take you hunting. How will it feel to try out your new atlatl? And what animals will you see on the hunt?

Grave Creek Mound was built by the Adena people in the region that is now West Virginia.

with bark or woven-grass mats. They also made pottery from clay they dug from the riverbanks.

Once people began to farm and make pots for storing food, they could settle down long enough to bury their dead in one place. From about 1000 to 500 BCE, a civilization called Adena did just that. They buried their dead in huge, earthen mounds, together with personal items such as stone pipes, copper bracelets, and clay pots.

Grave Creek Mound in Moundsville is the largest cone-shaped Adena mound in North America. It stands 62 feet (19 m) high and 240 feet (73 m) in diameter. Adena people began building the Grave Creek Mound in about 250 BCE. Over the course of a century, it grew higher and higher with new layers of burials. Criel Mound in South Charleston is the state's second-largest Adena mound.

At Adena settlements, **archaeologists** have unearthed objects made from surprising material—copper, grizzly

WORD TO KNOW

archaeologists *people who study the remains of past human cultures*

bear teeth, and shells. Why is this material surprising? Because the area didn't have copper, grizzly bears, or an ocean. Scientists have determined that the copper came from the Great Lakes, the grizzly bear teeth from the Rocky Mountains, and the shells from the Gulf of Mexico. The Adena people must have been part of a trade network that brought these goods to their settlements from faraway places.

By the year 1 CE, other Mound Builders were migrating into the West Virginia area from the Illinois River valley to the west. In some regions, they built stone burial mounds instead of earthen mounds. These Mound Builders, called the Hopewell people, constructed Murad Mound in Saint Albans and others in the South Charleston area. They grew corn, beans, squash, and various seed plants, and made clay pottery such as jars and bowls, which they decorated with geometric or animal designs.

THE FORT ANCIENT CULTURE

By about 800 CE, a new civilization had spread northeastward from present-day Missouri into West Virginia. Its people cultivated corn on such a large scale that they needed leaders for the project. They built cities with small, outlying villages. In the cities, temples and leaders' homes stood atop flat-topped, pyramid-shaped mounds. Priests conducted religious ceremonies, and both priests and leaders shared political power. This culture, called Mississippian, was strongest in the Ohio and Kanawha river valleys.

Around 1000 CE, people of the Fort Ancient culture began occupying western West Virginia. Their large, circular towns had an open plaza in the center, surrounded by square or rectangular homes with thatched roofs. Some home owners wove sticks through the wood-pole walls and

Hopewell pottery

Fort Ancient villagers lived in thatched homes like these.

smeared clay on them to keep the wind out. Walls of wooden stakes, called palisades, sometimes enclosed a town.

Fort Ancient villagers cultivated large fields of corn, beans, and squash. They caught fish and hunted deer and other wild game with bows and arrows. Instead of building burial mounds, they buried their dead in the ground, under their homes. People of the Monongahela culture lived farther north and east. They had a similar way of life, although their villages were smaller.

The Buffalo Site, a Fort Ancient village along the Kanawha River, was one of the largest Native American settlements in today's West Virginia. As many as 500 people may have lived there. Around the central courtyard stood large homes, some as big as 50 feet (15 m) long and 25 feet (8 m) wide. People buried their dead with jewelry, arrowheads, pottery, and carved pipes. Scientists who studied the villagers' remains discovered that they suffered from

Squash was one crop grown by the Fort Ancient people.

arthritis, tuberculosis, anemia (lack of iron), and other disorders. Some scientists believe that many of these diseases resulted from poor nutrition. They think that the population grew so large that people didn't get enough of the right kinds of food to eat.

Native American Peoples
(Before European Contact)

This map shows the general area of Native American peoples before European settlers arrived.

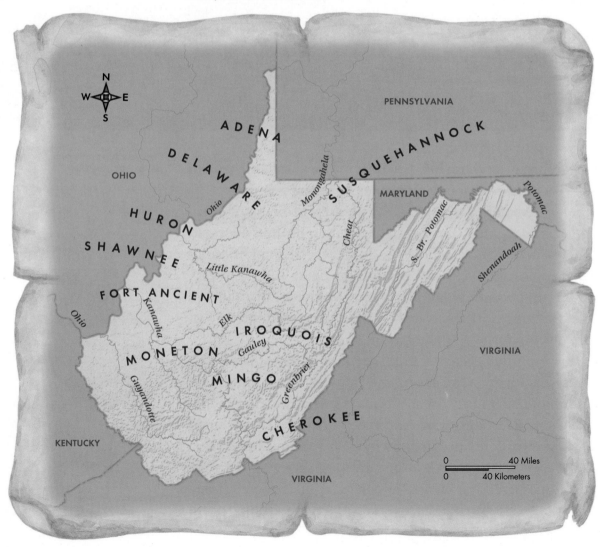

THE IROQUOIS CONFEDERACY

By about 1600, Shawnees, Delawares, Hurons, and other Native American groups had moved into West Virginia from neighboring regions. They lived in smaller settlements than the Fort Ancient people and relied more on hunting than farming. Most of these groups were not able to stay long.

In the 1500s, several Native American groups in present-day New York State had formed a powerful **alliance** called the Iroquois **Confederacy**. Around 1650, they began driving other groups out of West Virginia, including people of the Fort Ancient culture. West Virginia became a hunting ground for the Iroquois and groups under their protection.

Native Americans in the region noticed that deer and buffalo gathered at a saltwater spring along the Kanawha River to lick salt. The Indians collected **brine** and boiled the water away, leaving salt. Kanawha Valley salt would later become the basis of West Virginia's first mineral industry.

LATER COMMUNITIES

By the late 1600s, fewer Native people lived in West Virginia. The Shawnee people lived in the Kanawha River valley and had towns in what is now Greenbrier County. The Cherokee Nation claimed lands to the south of the valley. Monetons occupied a village near today's Malden. Land along the Ohio River from Parkersburg to Wheeling was a Mingo hunting ground. Delawares ranged along the Monongahela River valley, and Tuscaroras settled at the tip of the Eastern Panhandle.

Soon European settlers from eastern Virginia began trickling into the region. They brought further changes to West Virginia's Native people.

WORDS TO KNOW

alliance *an association among groups that benefits all the members*

confederacy *a group that is formed for a common purpose*

brine *water saturated with salt*

FAQ

Q8 WHICH NATIVE AMERICAN GROUPS FORMED THE IROQUOIS CONFEDERACY?

A8 At first, the Iroquois Confederacy was made up of five Native American nations: the Mohawk, Oneida, Onondaga, Cayuga, and Seneca. A sixth group, the Tuscarora, joined in 1720. The Iroquois Confederacy is also known as the Six Nations.

READ ABOUT

A settler's cabin
below the cliffs
of Seneca

1671

Thomas Batts and Robert Fallam may be the first Europeans to reach what is now West Virginia

1754–1763 ▲

The French and Indian War is fought

1768

The Iroquois and Cherokee people are forced to give up their land between the Allegheny Mountains and the Ohio River

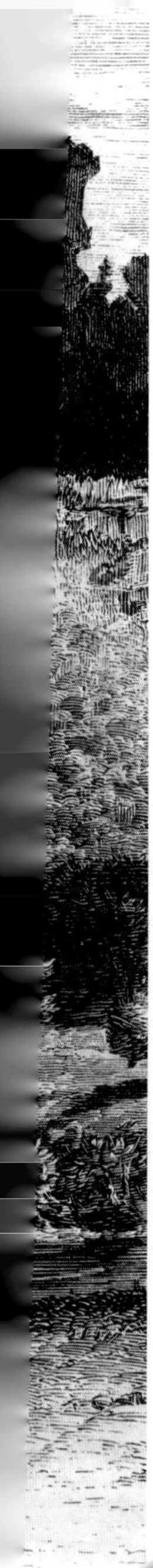

CHAPTER THREE

EXPLORATION AND SETTLEMENT

★

IN 1607, COLONISTS FROM ENGLAND ESTABLISHED JAMESTOWN, VIRGINIA, THEIR FIRST PERMANENT SETTLEMENT. In 1609, the king of England expanded their charter so that the Virginia Colony reached "from sea to sea"—all the way to the Pacific Ocean! Nobody really knew at that time all of what lay between the East and West coasts, but the charter opened the wilderness that became West Virginia to English settlement.

◄1774

Shawnee chief Cornstalk leads an attack at Point Pleasant

1775

Western colonists ask to establish their own colony, to be called Westsylvania

1788

Virginia—including today's West Virginia— becomes the 10th U.S. state

European Exploration of West Virginia

The colored arrows on this map show the routes taken by explorers between 1671 and 1742.

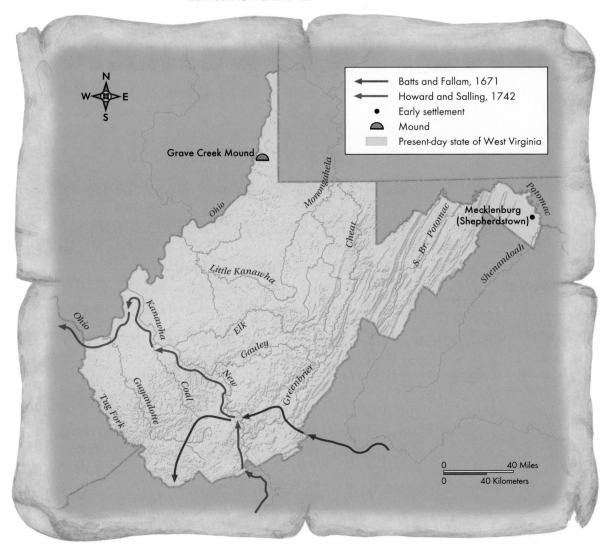

Batts and Fallam, 1671
Howard and Salling, 1742
• Early settlement
◗ Mound
Present-day state of West Virginia

Grave Creek Mound

Mecklenburg (Shepherdstown)

Ohio
Monongahela
Cheat
S. Br. Potomac
Potomac
Shenandoah
Little Kanawha
Kanawha
Elk
Gauley
New
Greenbrier
Coal
Guyandotte
Tug Fork
Ohio

0   40 Miles
0   40 Kilometers

VENTURING INTO THE WILDERNESS

Military leaders, fur traders, and land developers in the Virginia Colony all wanted to know more about the western frontier. Major General Abraham Wood hoped to build

Trappers hunted wildlife in the region in order to sell the valuable fur.

up the fur trade west of the Allegheny Mountains. In 1671, he sent Thomas Batts and Robert Fallam on a westward expedition. They may have been the first Europeans to venture into what is now West Virginia. Batts and Fallam reached New River and realized it was a tributary of the Ohio River. They claimed the right to trade and settle in the Ohio River Valley for England. France claimed the Ohio Valley, too, and this would lead to trouble later.

In 1716, Virginia governor Alexander Spotswood led an expedition over Virginia's Blue Ridge Mountains and into the Shenandoah Valley. He wanted to encourage people to settle there. These settlements would provide a protective barrier between colonists in the east and the

WOW

Governor Spotswood rewarded each of his expedition members with a miniature golden horseshoe encrusted with jewels. The men became known as the **Knights of the Golden Horseshoe.**

EARLY SETTLER

An immigrant from Wales, Morgan Morgan (1688–1766) settled on land near Bunker Hill in 1731 and built a cabin there. He worked as a road engineer, ran a tavern, and organized an informal local army. His son Zackquill founded Morgantown. Morgan's rebuilt cabin and Zackquill's house (seen here) are now historic sites.

WORD TO KNOW

Scots-Irish *an ethnic group consisting mainly of Protestant people from Scotland who began settling in northern Ireland in the 1600s*

French and Native Americans to the west. Spotswood returned with glowing reports of the valley's lush farmland.

The first European immigrants to make their homes in the Shenandoah Valley were German and **Scots-Irish** people from the Pennsylvania and New Jersey colonies. In 1727, several German families from Pennsylvania established a town called New Mecklenburg along the Potomac River. Now called Shepherdstown, it was West Virginia's first white settlement.

Soon Scots-Irish settlers and more Germans arrived. German immigrants were fleeing wars, forced military service, high taxes, and religious persecution. The Scots-Irish were fleeing religious persecution, too. With promises of religious freedom and other privileges, all were drawn to make new homes in the Shenandoah Valley.

In 1744, colonial officials purchased lands east of the Allegheny Mountains from the Iroquois Confederacy. By 1750, about 5,000 settlers were living in the Eastern Panhandle. Most lived in farming communities, while some made their living at industries such as blacksmithing, grain milling, and iron processing.

WARS, TREATIES, AND SETTLEMENTS

Throughout the Ohio River valley, conflicts were seething between France and Great Britain. (By this time, England and Scotland were combined as the kingdom of Great Britain.) Both countries claimed the territory. France wanted it for the fur trade, and Britain wanted it for settlement. These conflicts erupted into what is called the

French and Indian War (1754–1763). Because settlement was more of a threat to Native American life, many Indians sided with the French. The British won, gaining most of the land east of the Mississippi River.

Great Britain and its colonies still needed the Native Americans to agree to let people settle on that land. In the 1768 Treaty of Fort Stanwix, the Iroquois sold their land between the Allegheny Mountains and the Ohio River to British colonial officials. The Cherokee people, too, gave up their claims. This released a flood of white settlers into the region. They poured into the Greenbrier, Monongahela, Ohio, and Kanawha river valleys and other parts of the interior.

Troops crossing the Allegheny Mountains during the French and Indian War

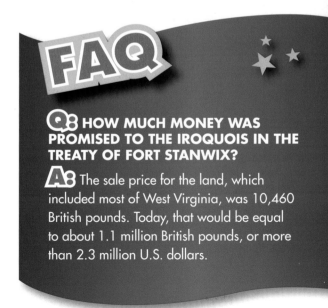

FAQ

Q8 HOW MUCH MONEY WAS PROMISED TO THE IROQUOIS IN THE TREATY OF FORT STANWIX?

A8 The sale price for the land, which included most of West Virginia, was 10,460 British pounds. Today, that would be equal to about 1.1 million British pounds, or more than 2.3 million U.S. dollars.

MINI-BIO

CORNSTALK: SHAWNEE LEADER

Shawnee chief Cornstalk (c. 1720–1777) hoped to protect Native Americans in the Ohio River Valley. His viewpoint was clear: Shawnee and Mingo people had never agreed to give up their land. Cornstalk led several raids on white settlers' towns. After settlers destroyed seven Mingo villages, Cornstalk was ready to fight back. In 1774, he led more than 1,000 fighters in an attack at Point Pleasant. After his defeat, he worked to keep the peace. White militiamen murdered him while he was on a peace mission to Fort Randolph.

? Want to know more? Visit www.factsfor now.scholastic.com and enter the keywords **West Virginia**.

WORD TO KNOW

militia *a group of citizens organized for military service, as opposed to a regular army*

Some Native Americans, especially Shawnees and Mingos, continued to resist settlement on their land. These clashes led to Lord Dunmore's War between the Virginia **militia** and the Indians. On October 10, 1774, in the Battle of Point Pleasant, the Virginians defeated Shawnee and Mingo fighters under Chief Cornstalk. This cleared the way for even more white settlers.

THE CULTURAL DIVIDE

Tens of thousands of people lived in the Virginia Colony by the 1770s. It was like two separate colonies in a way, because eastern and western Virginia had two distinct cultures.

In the east were "gentleman" planters who raised tobacco and other crops on large plantations. Large-scale farming demanded a massive labor force. To meet the labor demands, most planters owned enslaved Africans, who were forced to work the fields for no pay. At the coastal ports, shiploads of tea, cloth, and other goods regularly arrived from Great Britain. Upper-class people, who had grown wealthy from the tobacco trade, wore the latest fashions to their elegant parties. The colonial government was in eastern Virginia, too. Wealthy easterners controlled the colony's political and military affairs.

Life was much different west of the Allegheny Mountains. Settlers there had come from Europe or other colonies to scratch out a living in the mountains and hills.

Families in the mountains raised corn and other crops on small farm plots. They got much of their food by hunting bears, deer, rabbits, and squirrels. They also gathered edible plants in the forest. These small-scale farmers did not need slaves. The rough, hilly land did not support the type of large-scale farming that easterners practiced.

The westerners made clothing and other everyday items at home. For entertainment, they played fiddles and other instruments, often homemade, and sang favorite tunes from their homelands. They hunted raccoons, whose pelts were in high demand in Europe.

A colonial family harvesting crops on their small farm, mid-1700s

WOW

In 1769, a group of businessmen tried to establish a 14th colony named Vandalia, consisting mostly of West Virginia. Their motive was money. They hoped to buy cheap land and sell it for big profits.

SEE IT HERE!

PRICKETTS FORT

What was life like on Virginia's western frontier? You'll get a taste of that life when you visit Pricketts Fort in Fairmont. From April through October, you'll see costumed guides acting as frontierspeople doing everyday tasks that people did in the 1700s. They weave, spin, blacksmith, gunsmith, and make pottery. You'll also get a glimpse of Native American traditions and the fur trade.

THE REVOLUTIONARY WAR

Great Britain charged taxes on goods it shipped to its colonists, who had no representatives in Great Britain to approve or object to the taxes. This infuriated colonists, who began to demand "No taxation without representation!" In 1774, they formed a Continental Congress and began to discuss independence from Britain.

Meanwhile, colonists in the western regions, far from the coast, had their own set of complaints. They believed that their colonial governments ignored their needs, such as defense from Indian attacks. Westerners began to talk about forming a 14th colony, called Westsylvania. Westsylvania would include nearly all of today's West Virginia as well as small parts of Pennsylvania, Maryland, Virginia, and Kentucky. In 1775, almost 2,000 settlers from that region

Colonial leaders gathering at Carpenters' Hall in Philadelphia in 1774 for the First Continental Congress

Members of the Continental Congress preparing to hear the first public reading of the Declaration of Independence, 1776

signed a **petition** asking the Continental Congress to approve the new colony. But Congress ignored the request. The Revolutionary War (1775–1783) had begun, and the colonies needed to unite in the fight for freedom from Great Britain.

On July 4, 1776, while the war was still raging, Congress issued the Declaration of Independence. The colonies now called themselves the United States of America. That became a reality when the colonists won the Revolutionary War. One by one, the former colonies officially joined the new United States. Another appeal was made in 1783 to establish a state called Westsylvania, but again it was denied. Virginia—including today's West Virginia—entered the Union on June 25, 1788, as the 10th U.S. state.

WORD TO KNOW

petition *a request for some action, signed by a list of voters*

READ ABOUT

A view at the White
Sulphur Springs
of Greenbrier

1797

*Elisha Brooks builds a
salt furnace, beginning
the Kanawha Valley's
salt industry*

▲**1859**

*Abolitionist John
Brown leads a raid
at Harpers Ferry*

1861

*Virginia secedes from the
Union; western counties
refuse to secede*

CHAPTER FOUR

GROWTH AND CHANGE

★

AS THE 1800s DAWNED, SETTLERS IN WESTERN VIRGINIA WERE MOSTLY LIVING OFF THE LAND. They lived in log houses scattered throughout the wilderness. Charleston, today's capital city, was just a village on the Kanawha River. Industries developed more slowly in western Virginia than in the east.

1863 ▶
West Virginia enters the Union as the 35th state

1872
West Virginia gives African American men the right to vote

1912
Bloody conflicts break out between miners and mine owners

Inside a saltworks facility in West Virginia, mid-1800s

EARLY INDUSTRIES

Salt production was western Virginia's first big industry. It started in 1797, when Elisha Brooks put up a salt furnace on Campbells Creek in the Kanawha Valley. Following the method Native Americans used, he boiled the salty water until only salt remained in his big tubs. Others drilled deep into the ground to reach pockets of saltwater. They shipped salt to many other states, where settlers bought it to add to butter and to preserve meat. By 1846, the Kanawha Valley was one of the largest salt production centers in the United States.

In drilling for salt, people sometimes reached deposits of natural gas. This discovery led to West Virginia's natural gas industry.

Industrial centers rely on transportation to receive raw materials and ship out finished products. With a strong network of rivers and railroads, West Virginia was the perfect location for the budding iron and glass industries. An influx of Welsh immigrants who were skilled at processing iron helped make Wheeling a center for the iron and steel industries. West Virginia was rich in both the minerals and the fuel needed to produce glass. Glassmaking also took off, and soon Wheeling grew into a booming industrial city. By the 1850s, Wheeling was Virginia's second-largest city. Only Richmond, the state capital, had a larger population.

In western Virginia, slavery was not as common as it was in the eastern part of the state, but some farmers in the Eastern Panhandle used enslaved African laborers. And some of the new industries did, too. Both the salt plants and the coal mines had enslaved people among their workforces.

JOHN BROWN'S RAID

Settlers in western Virginia felt an ever-growing distance from Virginians in the east. Wealthy eastern planters controlled the state government, and westerners didn't get their share of benefits such as roads and public schools. Under pressure, the state held a convention in 1829 to iron out the problems. Westerners did get more benefits, such as broader voting rights, more state representatives, and better roads. But they still carried an unfair share of the tax burden. Tax laws favored slave owners because, in taxing a plantation according to its population, Virginia counted slaves at three-fifths of their true population.

Disputes over slavery were dividing not just Virginia, but the whole country. Some Northerners were **abolitionists**, while many more were opposed to extending slavery to western territories. Southerners who owned slaves wanted to preserve slavery.

On October 14, 1835, three white men and one white woman in Wheeling were charged with illegally teaching African Americans to read. This was against the law at the time.

WORD TO KNOW

abolitionists *people who were opposed to slavery and worked to end it*

JOHN BROWN: ABOLITIONIST

John Brown (1800–1859) was born into a deeply religious Connecticut family that opposed slavery. As an adult, Brown helped enslaved people escape, protected them, and gave them land. Although his raid at Harpers Ferry failed, his abolitionist dream lived on. A few years into the Civil War, northern soldiers marched into battle singing of John Brown, "his truth goes marching on."

? Want to know more? Visit www.factsfor now.scholastic.com and enter the keywords **West Virginia**.

SEE IT HERE!

HARPERS FERRY NATIONAL HISTORICAL PARK

This historic community spreads across the Virginia–Maryland–West Virginia border where the Potomac and Shenandoah rivers meet. It's built around the site where abolitionist John Brown led his 1859 raid. Through museums and exhibits, you'll learn about Brown, the Civil War, African American history, and life in the 1800s. Among the restored buildings are a jewelry shop, a clothing store, a dry-goods store, and a blacksmith shop.

U.S. troops breaking through the door of the Harpers Ferry arsenal

John Brown was a religious man committed to abolition, even if it meant he had to free Africans from slavery himself. In 1859, he led a band of 22 men that included 17 white abolitionists (among them his own sons) and five African Americans in an attempt to capture the federal **arsenal** at Harpers Ferry. He hoped to seize weapons and establish a colony where people fleeing slavery could live in freedom.

WORD TO KNOW

arsenal *a place where weapons are made or stored*

His plot failed, and most of his men, including his sons, were either killed or captured and executed. Only five escaped. Brown was executed, but he became a hero for many who opposed slavery. His execution stirred strong feelings in the North and South and helped bring about the Civil War.

THE NEW STATE AND THE CIVIL WAR

Tensions between North and South finally reached the boiling point. The Civil War began on April 12, 1861, when South Carolina troops fired on Fort Sumter in Charleston

Union soldiers at Harpers Ferry, 1862

West Virginia: From Territory to Statehood
(1763–1863)

This map shows the original West Virginia territory and the area (in yellow) that became the state of West Virginia in 1863.

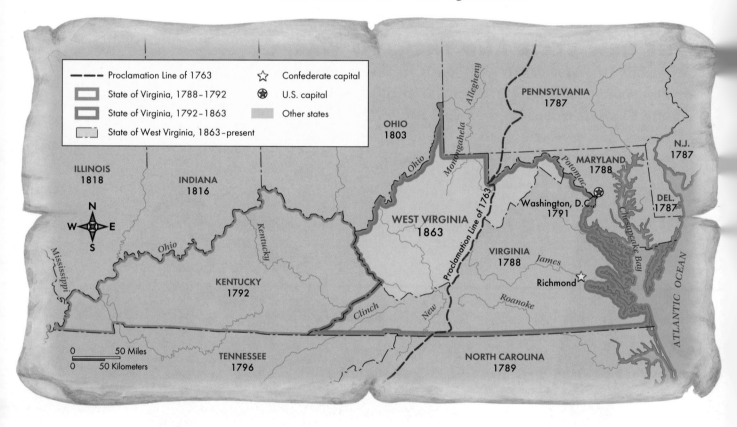

Harbor. Just five days later, Virginia voted to secede, or withdraw, from the Union. It joined 10 other Southern states in forming the Confederate States of America.

But in Virginia's western counties, most people didn't want to secede or fight for slavery. In May and June, their representatives met in Wheeling. At the Wheeling Convention, they voted to form their own state and support the Union. Delegates later drew up a state constitution that abolished slavery. West Virginia was admitted to the Union as the 35th state on June 20, 1863.

As Union and Confederate forces fought for control of West Virginia, the new state was torn by battles. Families and friends were torn apart, too. Most citizens supported the Union, but many West Virginians signed up to fight for the Confederacy. In fact, Thomas "Stonewall" Jackson of West Virginia became one of the Confederacy's leading generals.

Hundreds of battles took place in West Virginia, with victories on both sides. Union forces won the Battle of Philippi on June 3, 1861. Though just a minor battle, it's considered the first land battle of the Civil War. Confederate triumphs included occupying the city of Charleston for six weeks.

Railroads were especially important targets, since they carried military supplies. In northeast West Virginia, the Baltimore and Ohio (B&O) Railroad was a Union supply train. In southeast West Virginia, the Virginia and Tennessee (V&T) Railroad carried Confederate supplies. In the Great Train Raid of 1861, Stonewall Jackson captured B&O trains, disrupting the Union supply route. He also captured the Union arsenal at Harpers Ferry. However, Union troops managed to take back both properties.

MINI-BIO

THOMAS "STONEWALL" JACKSON: MILITARY LEADER

Confederate general Thomas "Stonewall" Jackson (1824–1863) proved himself to be a true military genius in the Civil War (1861–1865) at the battles of Bull Run, Antietam, and Fredericksburg. Born in Clarksburg, he graduated from the United States Military Academy at West Point and went on to serve in the U.S. Army during the Mexican-American War (1846–1848). When the Civil War broke out, Jackson sided with the Confederacy. He died after being accidentally shot by one of his own men at the Battle of Chancellorsville in May 1863.

? Want to know more? Visit www.factsfor now.scholastic.com and enter the keywords **West Virginia**.

WOW

It's said that during the Civil War, the town of Romney changed hands between Union and Confederate control 56 times!

JOHN HENRY, THE STEEL DRIVIN' MAN

John Henry is an American folk hero celebrated in stories, songs, and poems. According to legend, he was a tall, muscular, African American railroad worker. Supposedly, he worked in the 1870s on the Chesapeake and Ohio Railway in West Virginia. With powerful swings of his sledgehammer, he drove steel spikes into sheer-rock mountains to drill railroad tunnels. People called him the Steel Drivin' Man.

One day, a salesman showed up with a steam-powered drill. He boasted that it was good enough to replace the men. To save their jobs, John Henry challenged the steam drill to a contest: man versus machine. They would drill into Big Bend Mountain in Talcott. As the story goes, John Henry won, but he immediately died.

John Henry has become an enduring symbol. To many people, he represents the dignity of physical labor. But he also stands for the fate of workers who are replaced by machines.

WORD TO KNOW

segregated *separated from others according to race, class, ethnic group, religion, or other factors*

West Virginia's largest Civil War battle was the Battle of Droop Mountain on November 6, 1863. The Union army was trying to cut off the V&T Railroad route. The Union won, breaking the Confederates' strength in the state. The war dragged on for 18 more months, ending with a Union victory in April 1865.

WAVES OF NEW WORKERS

After the Civil War, West Virginia's coal, lumber, natural gas, petroleum, and manufacturing industries blossomed. Railroads were extended to transport raw materials and factory goods. Lured by the prospect of good jobs, thousands of immigrants poured into West Virginia. Most came from Italy, Poland, Hungary, and Germany.

Many African Americans left the South for jobs in the coal mines, too. Even though slavery had ended, they faced low wages and discrimination in the South.

In 1872, the leaders of West Virginia wrote a constitution that gave the vote to African American men, although it did not allow them to serve on juries and it barred their children from attending school with white children. But in West Virginia's coal mines, men of both races enjoyed equal pay for equal work. Coal companies provided housing for their workers, and although blacks and whites socialized separately, they enjoyed equal housing. Their children also had equal opportunities for an education, but in **segregated** schools. In some mining areas, a greater percentage of black children attended school than white children. By 1920, almost 70 percent of the African Americans in Appalachia lived in West Virginia.

By 1918, African Americans had been elected to the state legislature. Others promoted racial justice through African American newspapers. In the years that followed, black West Virginians built churches and joined groups such as the National Association for the Advancement of Colored People (NAACP) that fought for racial equality. Memphis Tennessee Garrison, a black teacher who lived from 1890 to 1988, devoted great efforts to winning justice for her people as a **civil rights** leader.

WORD TO KNOW

civil rights *basic human rights that all citizens in a society are entitled to, such as the right to vote*

Children playing outside the Pleasant Green School near Marlinton, 1921

CARTER G. WOODSON: FATHER OF BLACK HISTORY

Carter G. Woodson (1875–1950) worked as a coal miner in Fayette County, studying whenever he could. Ultimately, he earned a doctorate from Harvard University. Woodson wrote many books on black history, because he knew most history books did not tell about African Americans' significant contributions to American culture and history. In 1926, he started Negro History Week to promote the study of African American life in schools and colleges. It has since expanded to the entire month of February. Because he pioneered this field, Woodson is known as the father of Black History.

? Want to know more? Visit www.factsfor now.scholastic.com and enter the keywords **West Virginia**.

Picture Yourself . . .

Working in a Coal Mine

Suppose you are a nine-year-old living in southern West Virginia in the late 1800s. You don't go to school. Instead, because your family is poor, you work in the coal mines. Crouched between two machines—the coal breakers and the washers—you pick out pieces of slate and other waste as the chunks of coal rush by. Your slightly older brother works in the depths of the mine as a trapper boy. Standing ankle-deep in mud, he waits for a mule to come along hauling a cart of raw coal. Then he opens a trapdoor for the mule to pass through and shuts it again. Your workday may be as long as 14 hours. For this, you get 60 cents a day. When work is done, you are covered with soot from head to toe. You wearily stagger home and rest up for another day.

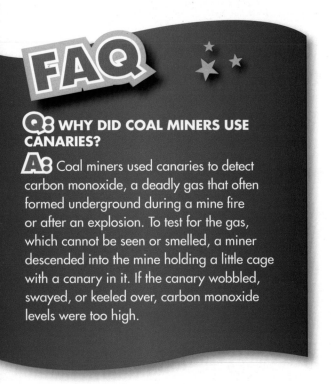

FAQ

Q: WHY DID COAL MINERS USE CANARIES?

A: Coal miners used canaries to detect carbon monoxide, a deadly gas that often formed underground during a mine fire or after an explosion. To test for the gas, which cannot be seen or smelled, a miner descended into the mine holding a little cage with a canary in it. If the canary wobbled, swayed, or keeled over, carbon monoxide levels were too high.

MINING STRUGGLES

Working in the mines was dangerous. Miners faced cave-ins, explosions, floods, and fires. Some fell down mine shafts, and others were crushed when underground roofs and walls caved in. There were frequent explosions in the mines, often followed by fires. Men might escape such instant disasters only to suffer later in life from black lung disease after years of breathing coal dust.

Living conditions for miners presented problems, too. The coal companies built their own towns, with company housing and a company store. Wages were low, and miners had to pay rent for their housing and mining supplies. If a miner needed an advance on his paycheck, he was issued a paper slip or metal token called "scrip" that could be spent only at the company store. The amount was then deducted from his next paycheck. Some companies even paid their workers in scrip instead of money. Many miners spent their lives in debt to the store, so they could never leave their jobs. The coal-mining song "Sixteen Tons" expressed their predicament: "Saint Peter, don't you call me, 'cause I can't go / I owe my soul to the company store."

In 1890, miners in Ohio organized a labor union called the United Mine Workers of America (UMWA). Through the union, miners

Workers prepare for a 10-hour day in a Gary coal mine, 1908

could bargain as a group for better wages and work conditions. Union workers could also call a strike, or refuse to work, if their demands were not met.

The UMWA had trouble unionizing miners in West Virginia. Mine owners were too powerful and had many friends in law enforcement. A little white-haired woman known as Mother Jones was determined to change that. A fiery speaker and a brilliant organizer, she inspired hundreds of miners to join the union and encouraged them to strike. Thanks to Mother Jones's bravery, many West Virginia mines were unionized by the early 1900s.

MINI-BIO

MOTHER JONES: THE MINERS' ANGEL

Affectionately called Mother Jones, Mary Harris Jones (1830–1930) was a labor organizer who worked among West Virginia's coal miners. She took part in the labor struggles of miners, steelworkers, railroad workers, and many other labor organizations. She also brought attention to how child workers suffered and died in the mines. Jones was imprisoned several times. She called herself a hell-raiser, and an opponent called her "the most dangerous woman in America." But miners called her the Miners' Angel.

? Want to know more? Visit www.factsfor now.scholastic.com and enter the keywords **West Virginia**.

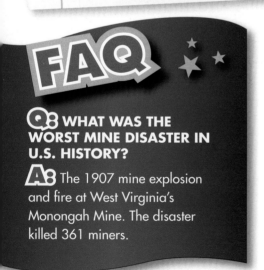

FAQ

Q: WHAT WAS THE WORST MINE DISASTER IN U.S. HISTORY?

A: The 1907 mine explosion and fire at West Virginia's Monongah Mine. The disaster killed 361 miners.

Mother Jones was on the scene when miners along Paint Creek and Cabin Creek went on strike in 1912. Their demands were not extreme. They wanted a small increase in pay so they could feed their families. They also wanted the right to free speech, to buy goods somewhere other than the company store, and to have their coal weighed without being cheated by the mine owners. But the mine owners refused, and the strike went on for weeks. Armed guards were brought in, and dozens of people were killed. Finally, the governor ordered the mine owners to negotiate with the miners.

INDUSTRIAL GROWTH AND WAR

By the early 1900s, coal was West Virginia's major industry. West Virginia was also the nation's top producer of natural gas and a leader in petroleum production. Manufacturing industries flourished, too. There were chemical plants in the Kanawha Valley, iron and steel plants in Wheeling and Weirton, shipyards on the Ohio and Kanawha Rivers, and glass factories throughout the state.

During World War I (1914–1918), several European countries waged war against one another. Once the United States joined the war in 1917, West Virginia's factories and mines turned out tons of supplies for the war

Workers building a ship in a Raymond City shipyard, early 1900s

effort. The U.S. government also built a massive plant in Nitro to make explosives and chemicals.

Tens of thousands of West Virginians stepped up to fight in the war. One of them was 14-year-old Chester Merriman of Romney, said to have been the youngest soldier in World War I. As young as he was, he showed typical West Virginian traits: loyalty, initiative, and willingness to meet a challenge.

READ ABOUT

Striking miners
and their families
in Ward, 1931

1921

*Mine owners and coal
miners battle at Blair
Mountain*

1950s

*Eighty thousand coal
miners lose their jobs*

▲1958

*People begin demanding
that businesses serve
African Americans*

CHAPTER FIVE

MORE MODERN TIMES

★

BY 1920, APPROXIMATELY 50,000 WEST VIRGINIA MINERS WERE MEMBERS OF A UNION. But the mine owners were determined to break the unions' influence. On May 19, 1920, gunfire erupted in Matewan between miners and armed detectives hired by the mining companies. This Battle of Matewan left several people dead. But the worst battle was yet to come.

1989 ►

Cecil Roberts Jr. helps
lead a strike against
Pittston Coal Company

mid-1990s

Mining companies
begin using
mountaintop removal to
extract coal

2010

Twenty-nine miners
die in an explosion
at the Upper Big
Branch Mine

State police and mine guards take on armed miners during the Battle of Blair Mountain.

BLOODY LABOR BATTLES

In August 1921, Mother Jones called on miners to march into Logan and Mingo counties and unionize the mines there. Thousands of armed miners from several states joined the march. Meanwhile, armed guards, state police, and federal troops gathered to stop them. Even U.S. Army bombers were called in. The miners set up a line of defense along a ridge on Blair Mountain. Someone opened fire, and the shootout lasted for days. As many as 30 people were killed, and hundreds were injured.

Called the Battle of Blair Mountain, this was the country's largest armed conflict since the Civil War. The miners lost the battle, and the union was severely crippled. Membership plummeted. Nevertheless, the battle brought the plight of miners to national attention and paved the way for labor victories in the future.

During the Great Depression, this worker from one of the New Deal programs lived on a riverboat with his family, near Charleston.

DEPRESSION AND WAR

The Great Depression of the 1930s hit West Virginia hard. This nationwide period of economic hardship left thousands of miners unemployed. The U.S. government's job programs, called the New Deal, put many people to work building roads, dams, and other public works. At the same time, new federal and state laws brought tremendous benefits to laborers. The National Labor Relations Act of 1935 gave workers the right to organize labor unions. The Wages and Hours Act of 1938 limited the workweek to 44 hours.

World War II (1939–1945) brought about an industrial boom for the state. Record numbers of West Virginians went to work in mines and factories to produce iron, steel, coal, chemicals, ammunition, and other supplies for the war effort.

ECONOMIC UPS AND DOWNS

After the war, most states enjoyed a new prosperity. But not West Virginia. Newly developed mining equipment began replacing thousands of workers. The demand for coal was dropping, too, as industries began using different sources of energy. As many as 80,000 miners were laid off in the 1950s, and West Virginia had the highest unemployment rate in the nation. West Virginians left the state in droves to find work in factories and plants in other states such as Ohio, Illinois, Indiana, and Michigan.

THE CIVIL RIGHTS MOVEMENT

Segregation was the rule in the state's elementary and high schools well into the 20th century. In 1954, the U.S. Supreme Court ruled that public schools must be racially integrated—that is, open to both white and black students. In West Virginia, most schools integrated fast. In 1958, civil rights leaders began protesting against restaurants, stores, and movie theaters that wouldn't admit African American customers. Like the schools, most of these establishments soon opened their doors to people of all races.

Some relief to the state's economic problems came in the 1960s. After President John F. Kennedy took office in 1961, his economic programs poured millions of dollars

MINI-BIO

HENRY LOUIS GATES JR.: SCHOLAR

Henry Louis ("Skip") Gates Jr. (1950–) was born in Keyser and grew up in Piedmont, where his father worked in a paper mill. In his book *Colored People*, he wrote about his experiences growing up during the time when African Americans were protesting segregation and other forms of discrimination. Gates went on to earn degrees from Yale University in Connecticut and Cambridge University in Great Britain. Today, he is a leading authority on black literature and culture. He has been a professor at Harvard University in Massachusetts since 1991 and chair of its African American Studies Program.

 Want to know more? Visit www.factsfor now.scholastic.com and enter the keywords **West Virginia**.

Students from West Virginia State College protest segregation in front of City Hall in Charleston, 1960s.

into West Virginia. Kennedy's successor, Lyndon B. Johnson, continued this trend with his Great Society programs.

In the 1970s, a nationwide petroleum shortage brought an increased demand for coal as a fuel. This boosted the coal industry and brought more workers into the state. But economic conditions in West Virginia seesawed. The 1980s brought high unemployment, and thousands of people once again left the state to find work elsewhere.

60

CECIL ROBERTS JR.: MINERS' UNION PRESIDENT

Cecil Roberts Jr. (1946—) grew up in Cabin Creek as a sixth-generation coal miner. Both of his grandfathers died in the mines. In 1989, Roberts led a successful strike against the Pittston Coal Company to keep health care benefits for retired coal miners and their families. He became president of the United Mine Workers of America in 1995. In 2005, he procured the highest pay raises for miners since 1974. He continues to work for better conditions and benefits for miners.

? Want to know more? Visit www.factsfornow.scholastic.com and enter the keywords **West Virginia**.

MINE SAFETY

Over the years, West Virginia's coal miners have faced constant challenges. Either they were unemployed, or they risked their lives working. Mining disasters claimed more lives every year. Some years were worse than others. Mine explosions killed 119 people in Benwood in 1924 and 91 people in Bartley in 1940. Mine safety laws helped improve conditions in the mines. But in 1968, a mine explosion in Farmington claimed 78 lives.

The public outcry after the Farmington disaster led to the Federal Coal Mine Health and Safety Act of 1969. It required several mine inspections a year, with stiff penalties for violations. Nevertheless, tragedy struck again in 1972. In the Buffalo Creek disaster, a dam holding back mining wastes burst. Millions of gallons of filthy black water gushed through Buffalo Creek. Within hours, 16 communities along the creek were wiped out, and 118 people were dead. This led to even more regulations.

Still, mining remains a dangerous industry and accidents continue. In 2006, a mine disaster in Sago took 12 lives. Federal and state investigations followed, and new regulations were put in place. Yet the harsh realities of mining remain. Coal miners' families still can't help but worry when their loved ones go off to work.

RECOVERY AND HOPE

West Virginia's economic conditions began looking up in the 1990s. State leaders worked hard to attract new businesses to the state. Computer software and other high-technology companies began to open offices along the highway between Morgantown and Clarksburg. This strip was nicknamed Software Valley. Thanks to the efforts of the late U.S. senator Robert Byrd, several government agencies moved their operations to West Virginia. In 1995, the Federal Bureau of Investigation (FBI) opened its Criminal Justice Information Services in Clarksburg. This facility became the FBI's national fingerprint center in 1999. The Internal Revenue Service opened a computer center in Martinsburg.

At the same time, the state faced serious environmental concerns. Electric power plants, which burn coal, released harmful gases such as sulfur into the air. Federal laws required them to reduce their emissions. Chemical plants released mercury into the streams, contaminating fish and posing a health hazard to the people who ate them. Mining operations have damaged the environment, too. Acids draining from the mines have polluted both soil and water. And some mining companies remove entire mountaintops to reach underground veins of coal.

The mining industry came under further criticism when an explosion in April 2010 at the Upper Big Branch Mine in Raleigh County killed 29 miners. The energy company that owned the mine was found guilty of many safety violations and illegal practices, and the company was forced to pay more than $200 million in fines.

A memorial to the miners who died in the 2010 explosion at the Upper Big Branch Mine

Since the 1990s, tourism has been a fast-growing industry in West Virginia. People around the country are discovering the state's natural beauty. In 2010, tourists spent more than $4 billion in West Virginia. The state's forested hills, rushing rivers, and other natural resources are major attractions. With luck, hard work, and wise decision-making, West Virginia can preserve these resources for generations to come.

Mountaintop Removal— Benefit or Disaster?

Traditionally, miners have extracted coal through underground tunnels. A mining method called mountaintop removal began in the mid-1990s. It involves blasting the soil off a mountaintop with dynamite to expose the underlying coal. Mining companies say it's a cheaper, safer way to mine coal. But local residents say it destroys the environment, ruins the landscape, and causes health problems.

Pro:

"Mountaintop mining operations produce desirable, high-wage jobs that are the economic engine of local communities, states, and the region in which they operate. The average mining wage is 57 percent higher than the average for industrial jobs. Mountaintop mining accounts for approximately 45 percent of the entire state's coal production in West Virginia. . . . Eliminating mountaintop removal will have a devastating economic impact on the communities where these mines are located."
—*Mountaintop Mining Fact Book*, the National Mining Association, March 2009

Con:

"Mountaintop removal exacts a heavy toll in both environmental and social costs. The practice literally flattens mountains and transforms densely forested mountaintops to treeless terraces and plateaus. . . . Residents are subjected to flash floods, polluted drinking water, lung-clogging dust, and the never-ending noise created by explosions at the mining operations, many of which operate 24 hours a day, seven days a week."
—*Mountaintop Removal*, by Sandra Zellmer, Center for Progressive Reform, 2009

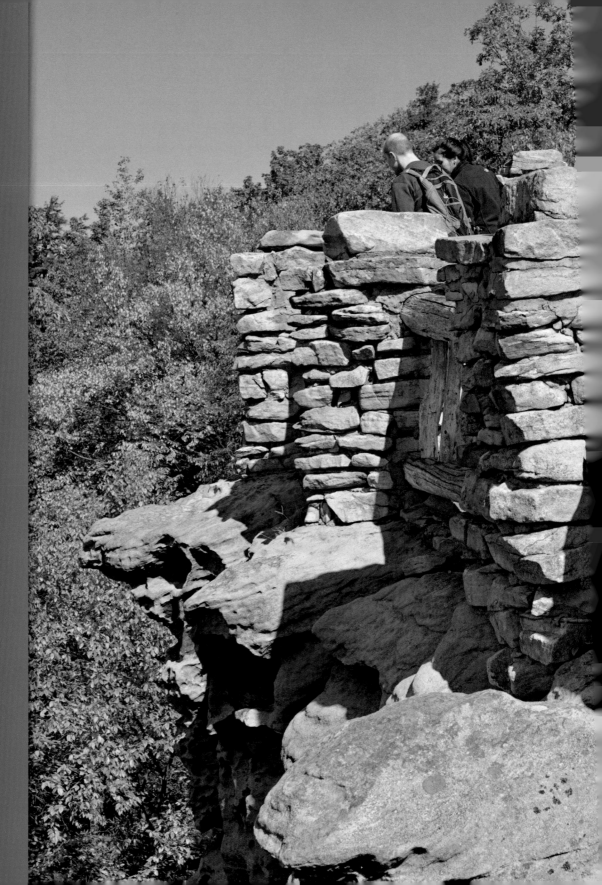

READ ABOUT

Hikers at Coopers
Rock State Forest

CHAPTER SIX

PEOPLE

★

THE PEOPLE OF WEST VIRGINIA SHARE A HISTORY OF STRUGGLE, HARD WORK, AND CHANGING TIMES. They reflect that history in their toughness, self-reliance, and independent lifestyles. West Virginians proudly preserve their historic traditions. At the same time, they welcome newcomers who seek the freedoms they value so highly. After all, as the state motto says, "Mountaineers are always free."

People from a variety of backgrounds call West Virginia home.

THE PEOPLE OF WEST VIRGINIA

Among all the states, West Virginia has the lowest percentage of foreign-born residents. Most West Virginians are descended from Europeans. Of those, most people report German, Scots-Irish, and English ancestors. Even so, the state is home to people of many ethnic backgrounds.

West Virginia's Metro Valley reflects the state's greatest ethnic diversity. This is the location of the state's biggest cities, Charleston and Huntington. The valley is home to West Virginia's largest communities of Filipino, Hungarian, Norwegian, Swedish, and Thai people. Chinese, Italian, Polish, and Russian communities flourish, too.

Many people with roots in India live in the Charleston and Huntington areas. Charleston's annual India Heritage Fair showcases Indian foods, music, and dance. Japanese people began moving into the Metro Valley in the 1990s to work for Japanese companies that have opened plants in West Virginia, including Toyota, which makes cars, and Kureha, which makes plastics.

A statue near the Clarksburg courthouse honors Belgian, Czech, Greek, Hungarian, Irish, Italian, Romanian, and Spanish immigrants. Many immigrant workers settled in the Clarksburg area after the Civil War. They were attracted to the region's industries, such as glassmaking and coal mining. Artisans from Belgium were a major asset in developing Clarksburg's glass industry. Italian immigrants came to work in both the coal mines and the glass factories.

Big City Life

This list shows the population of West Virginia's biggest cities.

Charleston 51,400
Huntington 49,138
Parkersburg 31,492
Morgantown 29,660
Wheeling 28,486

Source: U.S. Census Bureau, 2010 census

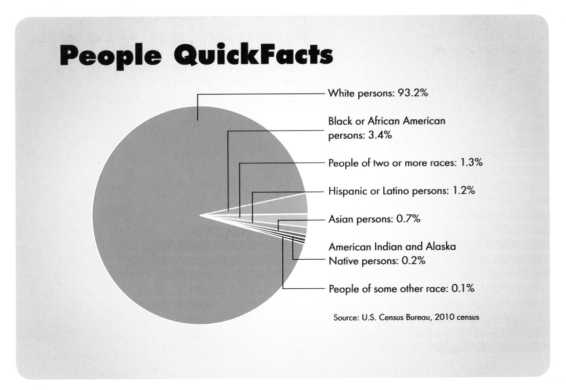

People QuickFacts

White persons: 93.2%

Black or African American persons: 3.4%

People of two or more races: 1.3%

Hispanic or Latino persons: 1.2%

Asian persons: 0.7%

American Indian and Alaska Native persons: 0.2%

People of some other race: 0.1%

Source: U.S. Census Bureau, 2010 census

Much of the state's Hispanic population lives in the Clarksburg area. There is also a growing community in the Eastern Panhandle, such as Berkeley and Jefferson counties. These two counties are home to 29 percent of the state's total Hispanic population. Many of West Virginia's Hispanic residents are migrant workers from Mexico who harvest fruit in the state's orchards. Others open small businesses such as day-care centers, groceries, and beauty shops.

After the Civil War, many African Americans moved into West Virginia. They came to work in the coal mines and built communities in mining regions. Today, most of the state's African Americans live in larger cities such as Charleston, Huntington, Wheeling, and Beckley.

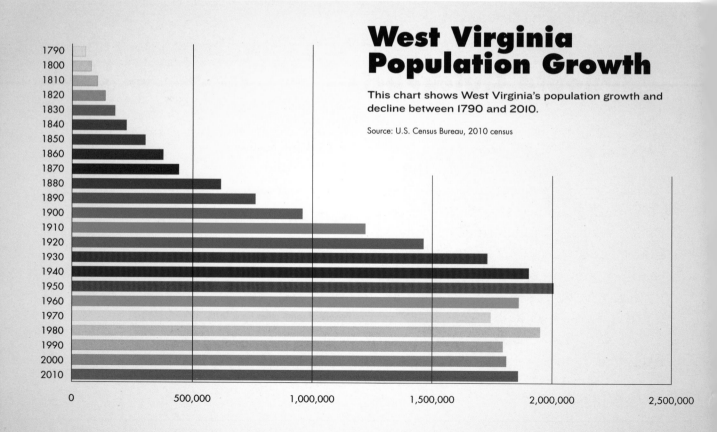

West Virginia Population Growth

This chart shows West Virginia's population growth and decline between 1790 and 2010.

Source: U.S. Census Bureau, 2010 census

Swiss immigrants settled in central West Virginia in 1869. They named their town Helvetia, the original name for Switzerland. Today, many residents of Helvetia still speak Schweitzerdeutsch, the Swiss-German language of their ancestors.

Immigrants from Wales helped build Wheeling into a center for the iron and steel industries. Today, only a small percentage of Wheeling's population claims Welsh ancestry.

The number of citizens with roots in the Middle East has more than doubled since 1980. Today the Arab population in West Virginia is among the fastest-growing Arab populations in the country. Many Middle Easterners live in Wheeling.

RURAL LIFE

West Virginia is one of the most rural of all the states. In 2010, 51 percent of West Virginians lived in rural areas, outside of cities and towns. That makes it the third most rural state in the nation. Over many generations, rural West Virginians have developed a unique folk culture. One example can be found in the Coal River valley of southwestern West Virginia. Homes are nestled in hilly forestland, which functions as a commons—land shared and used by the whole community. Many people in the Coal River valley still hunt deer, bears, squirrels, and wild turkeys and fish in the creeks and streams.

Community events reinforce shared values and common bonds. People hold family reunions and group dinners, cookouts, and fish fries. They meet for storytelling sessions and musical get-togethers with fiddles, banjos, and harmonicas. In some places, the whole community comes together for labor-heavy activities such as making molasses.

SEE IT HERE!

FASNACHT IN HELVETIA

Residents of Helvetia still celebrate the ancient festival of Fasnacht. Similar to Mardi Gras, Fasnacht takes place usually in late February, on the last Saturday before the Christian observance of Ash Wednesday and the solemn pre-Easter season of Lent. Fasnacht has its roots in Switzerland's Winterfest. People wear elaborate costumes with large, scary masks. After a parade, they burn an **effigy** of Old Man Winter in a huge bonfire to signal the end of winter and the coming of spring.

WORD TO KNOW

effigy *a model; usually a large, clothed dummy that is filled with stuffing*

Where West Virginians Live

The colors on this map indicate population density throughout the state. The darker the color, the more people live there.

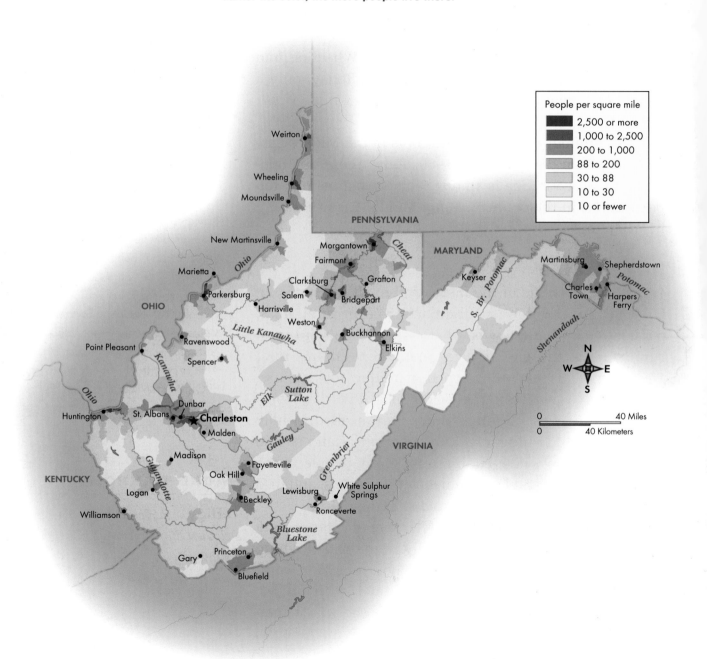

People per square mile

- 2,500 or more
- 1,000 to 2,500
- 200 to 1,000
- 88 to 200
- 30 to 88
- 10 to 30
- 10 or fewer

PENNSYLVANIA

MARYLAND

OHIO

KENTUCKY

VIRGINIA

Weirton

Wheeling

Moundsville

New Martinsville

Marietta

Parkersburg

Harrisville

Point Pleasant

Ravenswood

Spencer

Morgantown

Fairmont

Clarksburg

Salem

Weston

Grafton

Bridgeport

Buckhannon

Elkins

Keyser

Martinsburg

Shepherdstown

Charles Town

Harpers Ferry

Huntington

St. Albans

Dunbar

Charleston

Malden

Madison

Logan

Williamson

Oak Hill

Fayetteville

Beckley

Lewisburg

White Sulphur Springs

Roncerverte

Gary

Princeton

Bluefield

Ohio

Little Kanawha

Kanawha

Ohio

Guyandotte

Elk

Sutton Lake

Gauley

Greenbrier

Bluestone Lake

Cheat

S. Br. Potomac

Potomac

Shenandoah

N
W E
S

0   40 Miles
0   40 Kilometers

Students on the Marshall University campus

EDUCATION

Children in West Virginia are required to attend school from ages 6 through 17. Most schoolchildren go to state-supported public schools. Only about 1 in 20 students is enrolled in private school. Students can also take online courses, either as individuals or as members of classes, through the West Virginia Virtual School.

West Virginia has more than 40 colleges and universities. Public schools include West Virginia University (WVU) in Morgantown and Marshall University in Huntington. Private institutions include Bethany College in Bethany, West Virginia Wesleyan College in Buckhannon, and Davis & Elkins College in Elkins.

THE GOLDEN HORSESHOE

Would you like to win a golden horseshoe? That's what eighth-graders in West Virginia try for. All year, they study West Virginia's history, geography, government, economy, and current events. Then they take an exam on these subjects. Students with the top scores in each county are presented with Golden Horseshoe pins.

In the 1700s, a group of men explored the little-known lands beyond the Allegheny Mountains. Upon their return, each one received a golden horseshoe, and they became known as Knights of the Golden Horseshoe. Like the knights, the students have made their own explorations of West Virginia.

HOW TO TALK LIKE A WEST VIRGINIAN

In mountain communities, people use a folk speech common to other Appalachian regions. It uses many terms passed down from early English and Scots-Irish settlers. If you say you've been "a-studyin'," for example, you are using language spoken by Scots-Irish people hundreds of years ago. Something that curves or bulges out is said to "pooch out." That *pooch* is a Scottish variation of the word *pouch*. German settlers are said to have introduced the word *briggity*, or *biggity*, meaning "self-centered." Someone with a big ego is called "briggity britches." Today, researchers are studying the wealth of historical information that West Virginians preserve in their speech patterns.

HOW TO EAT LIKE A WEST VIRGINIAN

Like people throughout Appalachia, West Virginians traditionally eat things they raise, catch, or make themselves. Fried chicken, ham, and sausage are typical meats. Corn bread, mashed potatoes, and fresh beans, squash, cucumbers, and tomatoes round out a hearty meal. Apple butter, buckwheat cakes, and fruit or berry pie are favorites, too. Some West Virginians roam the woods to find special foods. In the springtime, they hunt for ramps (native wild onions) and molly moochers (morel mushrooms). They take the roots or bark of the sassafras tree and boil them to make hearty, red sassafras tea.

Corn bread

MENU

WHAT'S ON THE MENU IN WEST VIRGINIA?

★ ★ ★

Golden Delicious apples

Golden Delicious Apples

Golden Delicious apples were developed by one of West Virginia's own farmers. People use them to make applesauce, apple pie, and apple cider. Apple butter is a West Virginia favorite, and several towns hold apple butter festivals.

Pepperoni Rolls

Pepperoni rolls are soft bread rolls with pepperoni baked in the middle. Some also have cheese, tomato sauce, and peppers inside. Supposedly, Giuseppe Argiro invented pepperoni rolls in 1927 in Fairmont, West Virginia, the Pepperoni Roll Capital of the World. In any case, pepperoni rolls were a common food for coal miners in the early 1900s.

Ramps

Ramps are wild leeks, a type of onion, with a strong smell and taste. People pick them in the woods, especially in the mountains. They boil the ramps and then fry them in bacon grease. Some people make ramp vinegar, ramp jelly, pickled ramps, ramp pie, ramp salad, and even ramp wine. Richwood claims to be the Ramp Capital of the World. It's the home of the National Ramp Association. Hundreds of ramp lovers show up for Richwood's ramp festival in April. Many towns hold ramp suppers, too.

Ramps

TRY THIS RECIPE
Applesauce

For this recipe, you can use West Virginia's favorite apple, the Golden Delicious, but many other varieties of apple will work as well. Be sure to have an adult nearby to help.

Ingredients:
2 large apples
a pinch each of cinnamon and nutmeg
1 tablespoon brown sugar (optional)

Instructions:
1.   Peel and core the apples and place them in a microwave-safe dish. Cover the dish loosely with plastic wrap.
2.   Microwave for about 3 minutes, or until the apples are very soft when you poke them with a fork. Allow the dish to rest for about 5 minutes, and then carefully lift the plastic wrap.
3.   Mash the apples with a fork or a ricer. Sprinkle the mashed apples with cinnamon and nutmeg, if you like. Keep mashing until it looks like applesauce.
4.   Add the brown sugar and stir. The applesauce is delicious served just as it is. You could also try mixing it with granola, serving it with ice cream or plain yogurt on top, or using it as a topping for pancakes or waffles. Makes 2 servings.

Dulcimer

PERFORMING ARTS

Appalachian folk music traditions are very much alive in West Virginia. They have been passed down from one generation to another since the days of English, Irish, and Scots-Irish settlers. With few outside influences, West Virginians in remote mountain regions have preserved their art forms for hundreds of years.

Fiddlers and banjo players entertain at square dances, concerts, or spur-of-the-moment jam sessions. Other traditional musicians play mandolins, guitars, and dulcimers. The dulcimer is a stringed instrument that sits on the player's lap or on a table. The player strums it or hits the strings with little hammers.

Lively Appalachian fiddle tunes are perfect for the fancy footwork involved in clogging and flatfoot dancing. Both are Appalachian folk-dance styles that grew out of English and Irish step dancing.

Before people had radios and TVs, they entertained each other by telling stories at home around the fire. Today, storytelling is a respected performance art in West Virginia. Some storytellers relate generations-old folktales, legends, and myths. Others recite stories found in books or tell about an unusual experience or event.

People also preserve folklore by singing ballads. Ballads usually tell a heroic or romantic story. Examples would be ballads about the folk hero John Henry or about a girl whose sweetheart went to war. Some singers keep up the tradition of shape-note singing, a song style that early colonists brought from England. The singers perform folk hymns with no instrumental accompaniment, reading musical notes written in different shapes.

Many festivals throughout the state feature traditional music and other performing arts. They include the Vandalia Gathering in Charleston, the West Virginia State

Bill Monroe and His Blue Grass Boys perform at a music festival in Summersville.

Folk Festival in Glenville, and the Appalachian String Band Music Festival in Clifftop.

Bluegrass, blues, country, jazz, and many other music styles have roots in West Virginia, too. The radio show *Mountain Stage* broadcasts live shows of a variety of music styles from its home in Charleston's West Virginia Cultural Center. Classical music lovers can attend concerts of the West Virginia Symphony Orchestra in Charleston and the Wheeling Symphony Orchestra.

Outdoor dramas are popular in the summer. One is *Honey in the Rock,* about West Virginia's birth in Civil War times. Another is *Hatfields and McCoys,* about the legendary long-standing hostility between two families. Both are held in Beckley's Cliffside Amphitheatre.

A West Virginia basket maker at work

ARTS AND CRAFTS

West Virginians proudly preserve their craft heritage. Local craft traditions include wood carving and glass-blowing. Wood-carving specialties range from furniture and walking sticks to musical instruments such as dulcimers. Some craftspeople specialize in spinning wool or weaving blankets. Others make baskets, pottery, brooms, rugs, or patchwork quilts. Broom makers use a stiff grass called broomcorn to make their brooms. Basket makers take a white oak log and split the wood into thin strips for weaving their baskets.

West Virginia has produced many fine artists, too. David Hunter Strother (1816–1888) of Martinsburg was a well-known magazine illustrator in the 1850s and 1860s. William Robinson Leigh (1866–1955) was born in Falling Waters and painted scenes of the American West. Blanche Lazzell (1878–1956) was a pioneer in modern art. Born in Maidsville, she received a fine arts degree from West Virginia University.

West Virginia's fine art museums include the Huntington Museum of Art, Parkersburg Art Center, and the Stifel Fine Arts Center in Wheeling. Many cities have glass museums that showcase the state's glassmaking history.

WRITERS

Many authors spent their early lives in West Virginia. Booker T. Washington was born into slavery in Virginia and grew up in Malden. His 1901 autobiography is titled *Up from Slavery*. Pearl S. Buck of Hillsboro spent much of her life in China, and her novel *The Good Earth* is about the life of a Chinese farmer. She was the first American woman to receive the Nobel Prize in Literature. John Knowles (1926–2001) of Fairmont wrote the novel *A Separate Peace* about a young man's high school days during World War II.

West Virginia has also produced many authors of books for children and young adults.

MINI-BIO

BOOKER T. WASHINGTON: EDUCATOR

Booker T. Washington (1856–1915) was born into slavery in Virginia. Free after the Civil War, he moved to Malden. At age nine, he began working in a salt plant and later worked in a coal mine. He managed to get a college education and went on to become the first president and principal of what is now Tuskegee University in Alabama. He became a distinguished educator and reformer. Washington wrote the story of his life in *Up from Slavery*.

? **Want to know more?** Visit www.factsfornow.scholastic.com and enter the keywords **West Virginia**.

BETSY BYARS: YOUNG-ADULT NOVELIST

When Betsy Byars (1928–) was growing up, she had two pet goats. She loved working with animals but planned to be a mathematician. Instead, she became a writer. She lived for 10 years in Morgantown, where she got the idea for her young-adult novel *The Summer of the Swans*. This book and her novels *Good-bye, Chicken Little*; *After the Goat Man*; and *The Midnight Fox* take place in West Virginia.

❓ Want to know more? Visit www.factsfor now.scholastic.com and enter the keywords **West Virginia**.

Julia Davis Adams (1900–1993) was born in Clarksburg. Many of her stories focus on the history of West Virginia. Her book *Stonewall* is about Civil War general Thomas "Stonewall" Jackson. Jean Lee Latham (1902–1995) was born and raised in Buckhannon. Her adventure tale *Carry On, Mr. Bowditch* is about sailor and mathematician Nathaniel Bowditch. Betsy Byars

Writer Julia Davis Adams was known for her books about West Virginia history.

lived in Morgantown for several years. She based her best-known novel, *The Summer of the Swans*, on her experiences there.

Walter Dean Myers was born in Martinsburg. His books, such as *Now Is Your Time! The African-American Struggle for Freedom*, focus on the African American experience. Beverly Van Hook (1941–) of Huntington is the author of the Super-granny mystery series. Cynthia Rylant (1954–) grew up in Cool Ridge and Beaver, and most of her books are about Appalachian life. Her novel *When I Was Young in the Mountains* is based on her own childhood.

MINI-BIO

WALTER DEAN MYERS: A WEST VIRGINIAN IN HARLEM

Born in Martinsburg, Walter Dean Myers (1937–) grew up in New York City's Harlem neighborhood. He bases many of his books on Harlem life and on the African American experience. Myers is the author of dozens of young-adult books, including *Somewhere in the Darkness* and *Now Is Your Time! The African-American Struggle for Freedom*. He often returns to West Virginia to visit relatives and research his ancestors' slave experiences at a plantation near Martinsburg.

 Want to know more? Visit www.factsfor now.scholastic.com and enter the keywords **West Virginia**.

SPORTS AND RECREATION

West Virginia's sports fans are proud of their Mountaineers. That's the name for all the athletic teams at WVU in Morgantown. Football and men's basketball are WVU's major sports. But there are Mountaineers who play baseball, women's basketball, men's and women's soccer, gymnastics, and many other sports.

The Mountaineers' basketball team reached the NCAA (National Collegiate Athletic Association) finals in 1959 and 2010 and won the National Invitational Tournament in 1942 and 2007. The Mountaineers' football team is outstanding, too. They won the 2006 Sugar Bowl, the 2007 Gator Bowl, and the 2011 Orange Bowl.

WOW

In 1960, 17-year-old Danny Heater scored 135 points in a Burnsville High School basketball game. That won him a place in the *Guinness Book of World Records* for the most points ever scored in a basketball game.

Basketball great Jerry West played for West Virginia University before he joined the Los Angeles Lakers.

Jerry West and Mary Lou Retton are among West Virginia's best-known world-class athletes. West, a basketball star, led the Mountaineers to the NCAA championships in 1959. He went on to play for the Los Angeles Lakers. Retton won the Olympic gold medal for all-around women's gymnastics in 1984. She became the first female athlete to be featured on a Wheaties cereal box.

For recreational sports, many West Virginians enjoy skiing, snowboarding, tobogganing, and ice-skating in the winter. When the weather is warmer, they may hike or hunt in the mountains or take to the rivers and streams for fishing, kayaking, canoeing, and whitewater rafting. After a carefree day of outdoor fun, they're sure to agree with the state motto, "Mountaineers are always free."

Fly-fishing in Tea Creek, part of the Monongahela National Forest

MINI-BIO

MARY LOU RETTON: OLYMPIC GYMNAST

When Mary Lou Retton (1968–) was four, she began studying dance and acrobatics in her hometown of Fairmont. Then she enrolled in a gymnastics class for children at WVU. At 14, she moved to Houston, Texas, for intense gymnastics training. Just six weeks after having knee surgery, Retton competed in the 1984 Olympics. She became the first American to win a gold medal for best all-around women's gymnastics performance. Now she's a motivational writer and public speaker.

? Want to know more? Visit www.factsfor now.scholastic.com and enter the keywords **West Virginia**.

READ ABOUT

West Virginia
delegates cheer at
the 2012 Democratic
National Convention.

CHAPTER SEVEN

GOVERNMENT

★

K IDS IN WEST VIRGINIA HAVE A LONG HISTORY OF TAKING PART IN THEIR GOVERNMENT. Since 1902, state leaders have been asking public school students to vote on the plants and animals that best represent West Virginia. Thanks to the students' votes, West Virginia now has the cardinal as its state bird, the black bear as its state animal, the sugar maple as its state tree, and the rhododendron as its state flower.

Capital City

This map shows places of interest in Charleston, West Virginia's capital city.

TOUR THE CAPITOL

The first thing you'll notice about the capitol is its dazzling golden dome. It's made of copper coated with gold leaf. Walk into the main hall, and gaze up at the two-ton chandelier. Sparkling lights bounce off its 10,080 glass crystals. Climb a sweeping staircase, and if the legislature is meeting, you can watch the lawmakers in action. Other buildings you can visit in the Capitol Complex include the Governor's Mansion, the Cultural Center, and the State Museum.

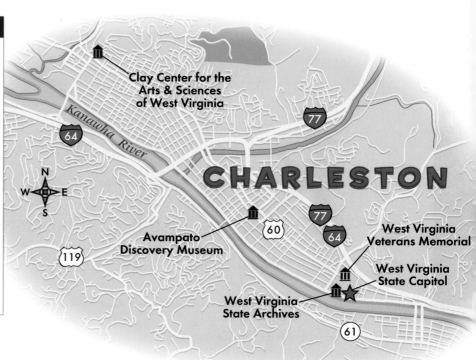

Capitol Facts

Here are some fascinating facts about West Virginia's state capitol.

Center building: 558 feet by 120 feet (170 m by 37 m)
East and west wings, each: 300 feet by 60 feet (91 m by 18 m)
Height of dome: 292 feet (89 m)
Number of stories high: 4
Floor space: 535,000 square feet (49,700 sq m)
Construction dates: 1924–1932

THE CAPITAL AND THE CONSTITUTION

Charleston is West Virginia's capital, or seat of government. That's where most of the important state government offices are. For years, the capital bounced back and forth between Wheeling and Charleston. Wheeling was the capital from 1863 to 1870. Then Charleston took over from 1870 to 1875. Wheeling was the capital again from 1875 to 1885. Finally, Charleston became the permanent capital in 1885.

West Virginia's constitution outlines its system of government and basic principles of law. The state adopted its first constitution in 1863 as a requirement for statehood. In 1872, a new constitution was adopted. Since then, West Virginians have updated the constitution with many amendments, or changes. The constitution calls for three branches of state government—the executive, legislative, and judicial branches.

West Virginia's capitol has the largest dome of all the state capitols. It's 4.5 feet (1.4 m) higher than the U.S. Capitol's dome in Washington, D.C.!

The capitol in Charleston

West Virginia State Government

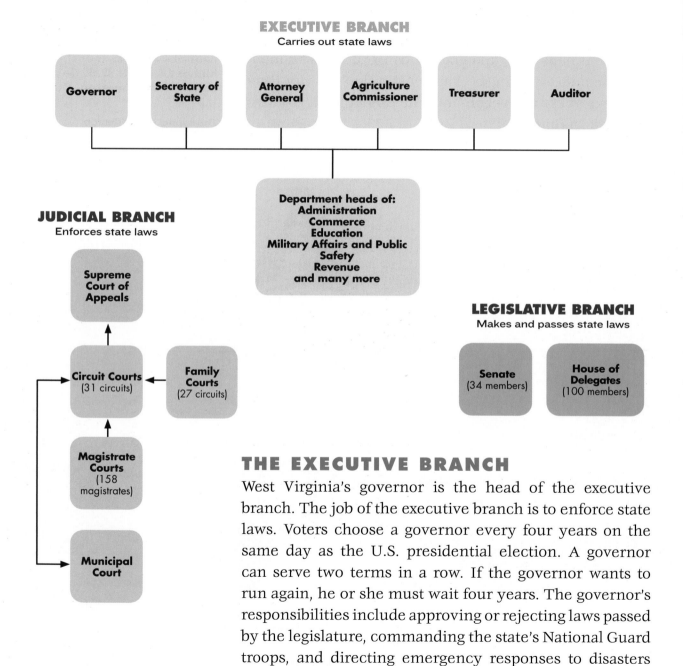

EXECUTIVE BRANCH
Carries out state laws

| Governor | Secretary of State | Attorney General | Agriculture Commissioner | Treasurer | Auditor |

Department heads of:
Administration
Commerce
Education
Military Affairs and Public Safety
Revenue
and many more

JUDICIAL BRANCH
Enforces state laws

Supreme Court of Appeals

Circuit Courts (31 circuits)

Family Courts (27 circuits)

Magistrate Courts (158 magistrates)

Municipal Court

LEGISLATIVE BRANCH
Makes and passes state laws

Senate (34 members)

House of Delegates (100 members)

THE EXECUTIVE BRANCH

West Virginia's governor is the head of the executive branch. The job of the executive branch is to enforce state laws. Voters choose a governor every four years on the same day as the U.S. presidential election. A governor can serve two terms in a row. If the governor wants to run again, he or she must wait four years. The governor's responsibilities include approving or rejecting laws passed by the legislature, commanding the state's National Guard troops, and directing emergency responses to disasters such as extreme weather.

Governor Earl Ray Tomblin signs a bill into law in 2013.

Most states have a lieutenant governor, who steps in if the governor is unable to serve. But West Virginia has no lieutenant governor. The president of the state senate takes on that role if needed.

Voters also elect several other executive officials. They include the secretary of state, auditor, treasurer, attorney general, and commissioner of agriculture. The governor appoints the heads of a number of departments. They're in charge of matters such as the environment, health, transportation, and taxes.

ROBERT BYRD: FROM THE COALFIELDS TO THE CAPITOL

Robert C. Byrd (1917–2010) was raised in the coal-mining region of southern West Virginia. As a young man, he worked as a gas station attendant, grocery store clerk, shipyard welder, and butcher. In 1958, Byrd, a Democrat, was elected a U.S. senator. As chairman of the Senate Appropriations Committee, he procured many benefits for West Virginia. At the time of his death in 2010, Byrd was the longest-serving member in the history of the U.S. Congress, having represented the Mountain State for 51 years.

? Want to know more? Visit www.factsfor now.scholastic.com and enter the keywords **West Virginia**.

The West Virginia house of delegates in session in 2012

THE LEGISLATIVE BRANCH

The legislative branch of West Virginia's government makes the state's laws. It's a bicameral legislature, meaning it's made up of two houses—the senate and the house of delegates. It's also a citizen legislature. In other words, serving in the legislature is not a full-time job, as it is in some states. West Virginia's legislators hold jobs in their communities and serve in the legislature part-time. When serving in the legislature, they meet in the capitol, a grand building in Charleston with a golden dome on top.

West Virginia's 34 state senators serve four-year terms. Voters in each of the 17 senatorial districts elect two senators. Their elections are staggered so that there's a senatorial election

Representing West Virginians

This list shows the number of elected officials who represent West Virginia, both on the state and national levels.

OFFICE	NUMBER	LENGTH OF TERM
State senators	34	4 years
State delegates	100	2 years
U.S. senators	2	6 years
U.S. representatives	3	2 years
Presidential electors	5	—

every two years. The 100 state delegates serve two-year terms. They're elected from 58 delegate districts. Each district elects from one to seven delegates, depending on how many people live in that district.

THE JUDICIAL BRANCH

West Virginia's judges make up the judicial branch of government. Their job is to hear cases and to determine if a law has been broken. The supreme court of appeals is West Virginia's highest court. Its five justices, or judges, are elected to 12-year terms. Every year, the justices choose one of their members as the chief justice. The supreme court of appeals hears cases appealed from lower courts. That is, someone who disputes the outcome of a case can call on the supreme court to review the case.

The state's 31 circuit courts handle serious cases. Each circuit court has one or more judges, who are elected to eight-year terms. On the county level, each county has at least one magistrate court. These deal with less serious cases. The magistrates, or judges, are elected to four-year terms. West Virginia also has family courts to handle divorces, child custody cases, and other family affairs.

LOCAL GOVERNMENT

Each of West Virginia's 55 counties is governed by a board of commissioners. Most county boards include three

MINI-BIO

JAY ROCKEFELLER: A LIFETIME OF PUBLIC SERVICE

John Davidson "Jay" Rockefeller IV (1937–) served the citizens of the Mountain State for nearly 38 years, beginning with his election to the West Virginia House of Delegates in 1967. The great-grandson of oil tycoon John D. Rockefeller, he served as West Virginia's secretary of state (1969–1973) and governor (1977–1985), as well as a U.S. senator (1992–2014). Rockefeller, a Democrat, was a strong supporter of the Affordable Care Act and an outspoken critic of violence on television.

 Want to know more? Visit www.factsfor now.scholastic.com and enter the keywords **West Virginia**.

A lawyer addresses the justices of the state supreme court of appeals about a mining case.

commissioners, whom voters elect to six-year terms. Other elected county officials include the sheriff, prosecuting attorney, assessor, county clerk, and surveyor of lands. They all serve four-year terms.

Most cities, towns, and villages elect a mayor and a city council. Some cities complain that the state government has too much control over the way cities operate. Under a program approved in 2007, cities with populations over 2,000 can try home rule. This allows a city to draw up its own charter, which is something like a city constitution. It gives cities more leeway in raising taxes, spending money, and making local regulations. In the Mountain State, the desire for independence lives on.

West Virginia Counties

This map shows the 55 counties in West Virginia. Charleston, the state capital, is indicated with a star.

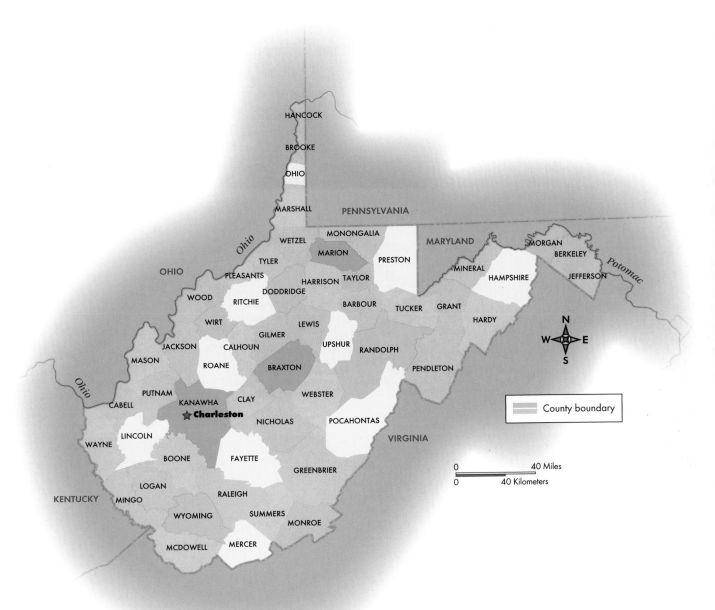

State Flag

The West Virginia state flag is a white field with a blue border and the state coat of arms in its center. The coat of arms includes the date the state was admitted into the Union and the Latin motto *Montani Semper Liberi* ("Mountaineers Are Always Free"). A banner reading "State of West Virginia" waves above the coat of arms, and a wreath of rhododendron hugs it from below. The flag was adopted in 1929.

State Seal

The stone in the center of the West Virginia state seal stands for strength. It reads "June 20, 1863," the date the state was admitted to the Union. Two rifles lie crossed in front of the rock. They are covered with a "cap of liberty." This symbolizes that the force of arms won and will be used to maintain freedom and liberty. On one side of the rock is a farmer with an ax, representing agriculture. On the other side is a miner holding a pick, representing industry. The seal includes the Latin motto *Montani Semper Liberi* ("Mountaineers Are Always Free").

READ ABOUT

A coal miner at work
in McDowell County

CHAPTER EIGHT

ECONOMY

★

FOR MORE THAN A CENTURY, COAL MINING WAS WEST VIRGINIA'S MAJOR INDUSTRY. In the mid-20th century, as coal mining declined, West Virginia became one of the poorest states in the country. So the state worked hard to develop new sources of income. Today, about three-quarters of West Virginians are service workers. They provide people with helpful services, rather than goods. But West Virginia is still a leader in producing coal as well as chemicals, metals, and other manufactured products.

These bakery workers are part of West Virginia's service industry.

SERVICE INDUSTRIES

Suppose you need to rent a canoe, find a Halloween costume, send a gift to your grandmother, or get a flu shot. For all these needs, you would go to a business in the service industry. Hospitals, schools, banks, restaurants, hotels, post offices, repair and rental shops, and ordinary stores all provide services. In West Virginia, most services are located in the big cities. Tourist services are very important to the state, too. Service workers have jobs in state and national parks, historic sites, and museums. They work in recreation areas where people go skiing, white-water rafting, and fishing.

Information technology is a fast-growing service industry in West Virginia. That includes computer software, Internet research, telephone communications, and other high-technology businesses. A stretch of highway from Morgantown to Clarksburg is known as Software Valley because so many high-tech companies are located there. It's also called the Interstate 79 Technology Corridor.

Government jobs are part of the service industry, too. Many national government facilities are located in West Virginia. They include the Federal Bureau of Investigation Fingerprint Center in Clarksburg and the Internal Revenue Service Computing Center in Martinsburg. In the 1950s, the National Aeronautics and Space Administration (NASA) opened the National Radio Astronomy Observatory (NRAO) in Green Bank. In 1962, the world's largest movable radio telescope began operating at the Green Bank observatory. Scientists use it to study distant space and learn about how stars form. The NASA Independent Verification and Validation Center is in Fairmont. It makes sure the space program's software works properly.

MADE IN WEST VIRGINIA

Chemicals are the leading manufactured goods in West Virginia. Several of the world's largest chemical companies, such as Dow and DuPont, have facilities there. Most chemical plants are located in the Kanawha Valley, especially in the Charleston area. They use the region's

MINI-BIO

E. M. STATLER: A BELLBOY WITH A DREAM

When he was 13, Ellsworth Milton Statler (1863–1928) began working as a bellboy in Wheeling's McLure House Hotel. By age 19, he was the hotel manager. He opened a restaurant nearby, where his mother and sister made sandwiches and pies. Statler dreamed of having his own hotel, and in 1907, he opened one in Buffalo, New York. Its selling point was "A room and a bath for a dollar and a half." This was the beginning of the nationwide Statler Hotel chain.

Want to know more? Visit www.factsfornow.scholastic.com and enter the keywords **West Virginia**.

SEE IT HERE!

THE NRAO SCIENCE CENTER

Green Bank's National Radio Astronomy Observatory (NRAO) has a fantastic science education center for kids. Tour the Science Center and try out its hands-on exhibits. Whether you're curious about radio waves from space or just enjoy stargazing, you'll find a lot to explore!

What Do West Virginians Do?

This color-coded chart shows what industries West Virginians work in.

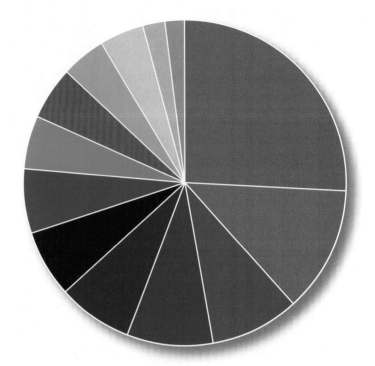

- **26.0%** Educational services, and health care and social assistance 198,013
- **12.5%** Retail trade 95,071
- **9.0%** Arts, entertainment, and recreation, and accommodation and food services 68,744
- **8.5%** Manufacturing 64,561
- **7.5%** Professional, scientific, and management, and administrative and waste management services 56,761
- **6.8%** Construction 51,384
- **6.4%** Public administration 48,452
- **5.4%** Transportation and warehousing, and utilities 40,884
- **5.2%** Agriculture, forestry, fishing and hunting, and mining 39,818
- **4.5%** Other services, except public administration 34,147
- **4.4%** Finance and insurance, and real estate and rental and leasing 33,185
- **2.2%** Wholesale trade 16,437
- **1.8%** Information 13,355

Source: U.S. Census Bureau, 2010 census

natural resources—such as coal, petroleum, and salt—to make dyes, medicines, plastics, and chemicals used in other manufacturing industries.

Metals are next in value. Plants in the Northern Panhandle produce iron, steel, tin, and aluminum. Other factories in the state make automobile parts, aerospace equipment, tools, and other metal products. The state's sawmills turn out lumber, and paper mills manufacture paper. Food plants process farm products to make baked goods and meat products.

An artist paints a new piece of finished glass at the Fenton Art Glass factory in Williamstown.

SEE IT HERE!

FENTON ART GLASS

You'll experience the glassmaking process up close at Fenton Art Glass in Williamstown. It's the nation's largest manufacturer of handmade colored glass. As you tour the factory floor, you'll see blazing furnaces melting the ingredients for glass. You'll see expert craftspeople blow through tubes to make rounded bubbles of liquid glass. Then you'll watch them spin and shape the bubbles into beautiful glass objects. Finally, artists decorate the glass with paints and gold.

West Virginia has a long history of making fine glassware. Glassmakers use local sand to make the glass, and they use local gas to fuel their fires. More than 500 glass factories once operated in West Virginia, many of them around Morgantown. Today, only a few glass factories are left in the state. They still make products such as glass bottles, fine crystal, stained glass, window and door glass, and table glassware.

Hancock County, in the Northern Panhandle, is a center for manufacturing clay products. The clay is made into bricks and tiles as well as china, porcelain, and other fine pottery items.

Coal miners head underground at a West Virginia mine.

MINING

In 2012, 538 coal mines were operating in West Virginia. A little more than half of them were underground mines, and the rest were surface mines. Marshall County, in the northernmost part of the state, produces the most coal. Boone County, south of Charleston, produces the second most and employs the most miners. Logan, Mingo, and Raleigh counties in the south and Marion County in the north are high-volume producers, too.

Although coal mining declined in the 20th century, West Virginia is still one of the nation's top producers of coal. Today, it produces more

Top Products

Agriculture Chickens, beef cattle, eggs, dairy products, turkeys, greenhouse and nursery products, hay, apples, corn, soybeans, tobacco

Manufacturing Chemicals, metals and metal products, lumber, transportation equipment

Mining Coal, natural gas, oil, crushed stone, salt, sand, gravel

coal than any state except for Wyoming. Most of West Virginia's coal is bituminous, or soft, coal. This type of coal is burned to produce steam that generates electricity. It's also baked to produce a substance called coke, which is used in steelmaking.

ON THE FARM

With West Virginia's rugged, mountainous terrain, it's hard for farmers to carry on large-scale agriculture with field crops. Raising animals is more profitable, and livestock brings in most of the state's farm income. Broilers (young chickens) are the top farm products, followed by beef cattle. Turkeys, eggs, and dairy products are next in value. Sheep, hogs, and goats are other valuable farm animals.

West Virginia's most valuable farm plants are nursery and greenhouse products. That includes potted and cut flowers, Christmas trees, and other decorative plants. In

WOW

It takes about 1 pound (0.45 kilogram) of coal to produce enough electricity to burn a 100-watt lightbulb for 10 hours!

Sheep on a family farm in Webster County

Major Agricultural and Mining Products

This map shows where West Virginia's major agricultural and mining products come from. See a cart of coal? That means coal is mined there.

Cattle
Chemicals
Coal
Dairy
Forest products
Fruit
Grains
Hay
Hogs
Iron ore

Mineral mining
Natural gas
Oats
Oil
Potatoes
Poultry
Salt
Sheep
Tobacco
Vegetables

Urban area
Forests, some farming
Farming

0   40 Miles
0   40 Kilometers

N
W   E
S

PENNSYLVANIA
MARYLAND
OHIO
VIRGINIA
KENTUCKY
VIRGINIA

Wheeling
Morgantown
Martinsburg
Clarksburg
Parkersburg
Elkins
Huntington
Charleston
Beckley
Lewisburg
Bluefield

Ohio
Monongahela
Cheat
S. Br. Potomac
Potomac
Shenandoah
Little Kanawha
Sutton Lake
Kanawha
Elk
Gauley
Greenbrier
Guyandotte
Bluestone Lake

some areas, people still gather food plants from the woods. In the southwestern mountains, ginseng root is an important cash crop. It's a medicinal plant believed to have many healthful effects, such as reducing stress. People also gather mushrooms in the woods.

A worker waters hanging baskets in a nursery greenhouse in Greenbrier County.

Hay is West Virginia's major field crop. Most of the state's hay and corn ends up as cattle feed. Soybeans, wheat, potatoes, and vegetables are some other West Virginia crops. The Ridge and Valley region, especially the Eastern Panhandle, has the richest soil for crops. A lot of farming takes place along the Ohio River, too.

Many farmers grow blackberries, blueberries, raspberries, and strawberries. Apples and peaches are the most important fruit crops. Two varieties of yellow apple—the Golden Delicious and the Grimes Golden—were developed in West Virginia. These juicy varieties make a great contribution to the apple lovers of the world!

GOLDEN DELICIOUS APPLES

In 1905, Anderson Mullins of Odessa discovered an unusual apple variety growing in his orchard. Year after year, it produced juicy, golden fruit. Mullins sold the apple tree rights to Stark Brothers Nursery in 1914. The Starks named the apple Golden Delicious. Now it's West Virginia's state fruit and one of the most popular apples in the world.

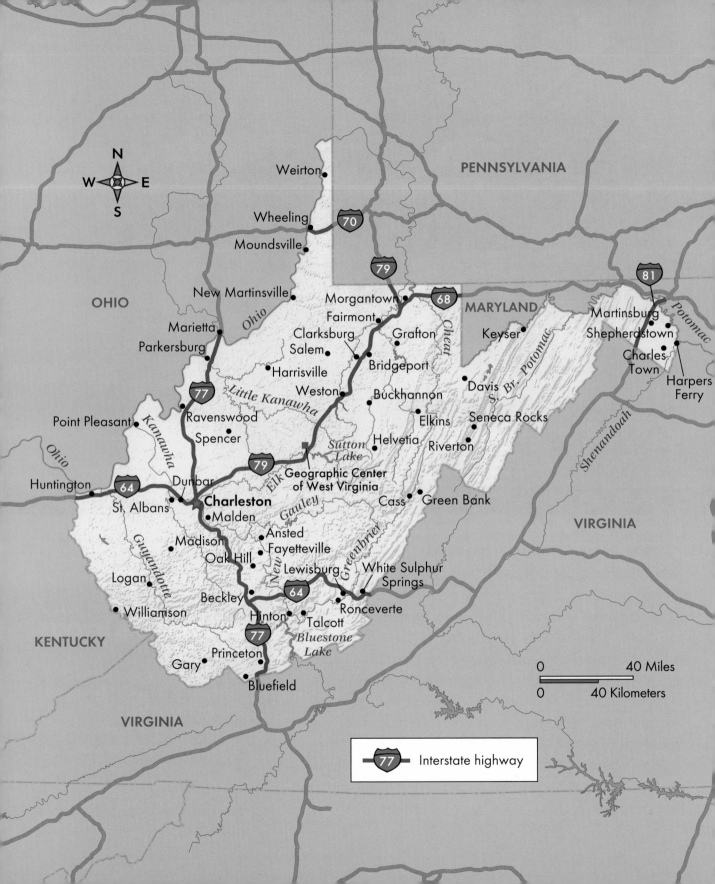

CHAPTER NINE

TRAVEL GUIDE

TRAVEL GUIDE

★

FROM ITS STEEP MOUNTAINS AND DEEP VALLEYS TO ITS CITIES AND VILLAGES, WEST VIRGINIA IS AN EXCITING PLACE TO VISIT. You can climb rocky mountains, descend deep into underground caves, or ride foaming river rapids. Or you can explore prehistoric Native American sites, Appalachian culture, and mining traditions. Whatever you enjoy, West Virginia's the place for you!

←—Follow along with this travel map. We'll start in Charleston and travel all the way to Harrisville.

METRO VALLEY

THINGS TO DO: Tour the state capitol, learn about the history of radios, wander through an 1800s farming community, or find out about the mysterious Mothman.

Charleston

★ **Avampato Discovery Museum:** Explore the world of science through dozens of interactive science exhibits. In the ElectricSky domed theater, you'll see giant-screen films and planetarium shows.

★ **State Capitol Complex:** When you tour the capitol, you'll gaze up at the largest state capitol dome in the country. Also visit the nearby West Virginia Cultural Center, the Governor's Mansion, and the Holly Grove Mansion.

War memorials at the State Capitol Complex

Malden

★ **African Zion Baptist Church:** Organized in the 1850s, this was the first African American Baptist church in western Virginia. Educator Booker T. Washington, who grew up in Malden, attended this church and, after college, began his teaching career there. In the reconstructed village behind the church are rebuilt versions of Washington's childhood home and early school.

Huntington

★ **Huntington Museum of Art:** On display here are paintings, sculptures, silverware, historic firearms, Appalachian folk art, Islamic prayer rugs, and many more unique pieces of art. The museum also houses the C. Fred Edwards Conservatory, a collection of unusual plants such as foxtail palms, Australian tree ferns, zebra plants, and golden shrimp plants.

★ **Museum of Radio and Technology:** See what radios were like in the 1920s, check out amateur shortwave radios, examine a working "crystal radio," explore military radio gear, and much more.

Point Pleasant

★ **West Virginia State Farm Museum:** This working farm is also a museum that preserves the state's farming heritage. Take a tour, and you'll find log cabins, an early farmhouse, a working blacksmith shop, doctor's and newspaper offices, and much more. Be sure to pet the farm animals, which include horses, chickens, donkeys, goats, and Sam the llama.

★ **Tu-Endie-Wei State Park:** A tall granite monument marks the site of the Battle of Point Pleasant. Called the First Battle of the Revolutionary War, it took place on October 10, 1774, between the Virginia militia and the Shawnee led by Chief Cornstalk. Also in the park is the Mansion House Museum, built as a tavern in 1796.

★ **Mothman Museum and Research Center:** A number of people in this area have reported sightings of a strange creature they call Mothman, a huge, humanlike figure with glowing red eyes and mothlike wings. At this museum, you'll learn all about Mothman and explore the history of Mothman incidents through drawings, newspaper clippings, and other exhibits.

NEW RIVER AND GREENBRIER VALLEYS

THINGS TO DO: Go kayaking, take a train ride through a coal mine, get a glimpse of traditional Appalachian life, or tour what was once a top secret government hideaway.

Fayetteville

★ **New River Gorge:** If you like outdoor adventures, this is the perfect spot for you. You can go white-water rafting, kayaking, or fishing in the river. The rough terrain around the river is great for mountain biking, rock climbing, or horseback riding. You can even take a mountain trek on a llama!

SEE IT HERE!

NEW RIVER GORGE BRIDGE

New River Gorge Bridge near Fayetteville is the world's second-longest steel arch bridge. That's a bridge with a curved arch between the end supports. This bridge measures 3,030 feet (924 m) from end to end, and the arch itself spans 1,700 feet (518 m). Only Lupu Bridge in Shanghai, China, has a longer span. (The span is the distance between supports.) On the third Saturday in October, hundreds of BASE jumpers from all over the world come to parachute off New River Gorge Bridge, 876 feet (267 m) above the river.

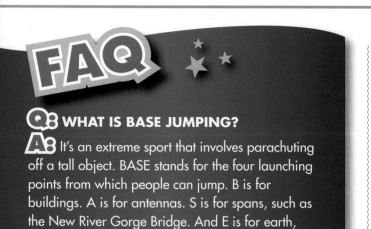

FAQ

Q: WHAT IS BASE JUMPING?

A: It's an extreme sport that involves parachuting off a tall object. BASE stands for the four launching points from which people can jump. B is for buildings. A is for antennas. S is for spans, such as the New River Gorge Bridge. And E is for earth, which usually means cliffs.

Ansted

★ **Mystery Hole:** Descend into this series of underground rooms, and the laws of gravity seem to go haywire. Water seems to flow uphill, and you can't stand up straight. See if you can figure out the mysterious powers of the Mystery Hole!

Hinton

★ **Saunders One-Room Schoolhouse Museum:** Do you like your school? You might like it even better after you see what school was like for kids in the 1800s. This museum is filled with reminders of old-time school days. You'll see antique desks, schoolbooks, and a potbellied stove that kept kids warm in the winter.

SEE IT HERE!

BECKLEY EXHIBITION COAL MINE

On the train tour through this mine, your guide is a retired coal miner who shares his knowledge and tells real-life mining tales. Near the mine is the Youth Museum, featuring exhibits on the region's history and culture, as well as a planetarium. The nearby Mountain Homestead re-creates a typical Appalachian settlement, including a one-room schoolhouse, log cabin, and weaver's shed with weaving loom and spinning wheel.

Beckley

★ **Tamarack:** At this shopping center, you'll find high-quality Appalachian crafts such as glass, pottery, hand-carved furniture, and quilts. You can watch artists give demonstrations of their crafts, too.

Talcott

★ **John Henry Monument and Big Bend Tunnel:** According to legend, this is the place where John Henry, the "Steel Drivin' Man," beat a steam-powered drill in a contest. A gigantic statue of John Henry stands at the top of the hill. Down below, you can explore the railroad tunnel Henry helped drill using only his sledgehammer.

Lewisburg

★ **Lewisburg National Historic District:** Stroll through this district and see the homes and shops of wealthy residents of the 1700s and 1800s. Lewisburg was an important agricultural center in this bluegrass-covered valley known as the Levels.

Ronceverte

★ **Organ Cave:** Tour this fascinating cave or even join an extended exploring expedition. It's one of the longest tour caves in the country, with more than 45 miles (72 km) of mapped passageways. In the 1790s, archaeologists discovered the remains of the first giant three-toed sloth ever found in the United States. Early Native Americans used flint from the cave to make arrowheads and other tools.

The Greenbrier in White Sulphur Springs

White Sulphur Springs

★ **The Greenbrier:** This luxury hotel has hosted presidents and royalty since healthful mineral springs were discovered here in the late 1700s. During World War II, the hotel was used as a relocation center for German, Japanese, and Italian diplomats. Then it was converted into a 2,000-bed military hospital. From 1959 to 1992, it housed a top secret, underground **bunker** for members of Congress in case of a nuclear war. The bunker was never used, and you can take a tour of the site.

WORD TO KNOW

bunker *a military defense fortification, usually located underground*

Williamson

★ **The Coal House:** This house was built in 1959, using 30 tons of hard, shiny coal! It's one of three known coal houses in the world, and all are in West Virginia.

POTOMAC HIGHLANDS

THINGS TO DO: Climb West Virginia's highest peak, explore underground caves, ride a steam train through the mountains, or tour a state-of-the-art astronomy observatory.

Davis

★ **Blackwater Falls State Park:** The park's sparkling waterfall is one of the most photographed sites in the state. This park is a great place for camping, hiking, fishing, cross-country skiing, mountain biking, and white-water rafting.

Biking in Seneca Rocks

SEE IT HERE!

BLACKWATER FALLS

Blackwater Falls tumbles 58 feet (18 m) over a rocky ledge into a deep gorge of the Blackwater River. The tea-colored Blackwater is dark because it contains tannic acid, a substance that comes from spruce and hemlock trees in the area.

Seneca Rocks

★ **Smoke Hole Caverns:** Over millions of years, the rock formations here were created by mineral-laden drops of water. Some of the formations you'll see are stalactites hanging from above, stalagmites sticking up from the ground, and helectites, which extend sideways.

★ **Seneca Rocks:** This series of high cliffs is a favorite challenge for experienced rock climbers. If hiking is more your style, you can follow a hiking trail to an observation area at the top.

Riverton

★ **Spruce Knob:** Hike the trail that circles Spruce Knob, and you'll reach the highest point in West Virginia. Signs along the way describe the geology, plants, and animals around you.

★ **Seneca Caverns:** Seneca Indians first used these caves around 1400 for refuge as well as for ceremonial rituals. Here you'll see a massive chamber called the Grand Ballroom and an underground pool called Mirror Lake.

Cass

★ **Cass Scenic Railroad State Park:** Hop aboard, and a steam-powered locomotive pulls your train through beautiful mountain country. It runs on the tracks of a former logging railroad. At one stop, you can get off and tour a reconstructed loggers' camp of the 1940s.

Visitors on the Cass Scenic Railroad

The National Radio Astronomy Observatory telescope

Green Bank

★ **National Radio Astronomy Observatory:** Scientists from around the world come here to study the sun, planets, and distant galaxies. They do it by analyzing radio waves from space. Take a tour, watch an educational film, and see the observatory's big, white dish— the world's largest fully steerable radio telescope.

Helvetia

★ **Swiss village:** Nestled in a valley, Helvetia is a Swiss settlement dating from the 1860s. Villagers are proud of their heritage and preserve many historic buildings in their community. Try some delicious homemade foods at the local restaurants and shops.

EASTERN PANHANDLE

THINGS TO DO: Visit the site in Harpers Ferry where John Brown staged his raid, see a model of an early steamboat, or stroll along streets that were bustling in George Washington's time.

Charles Town

★ **Happy Retreat:** George Washington's brother Charles, who founded the city of Charles Town, built this as his home around 1780. On the grounds are the mansion, a stone-and-brick kitchen and store-house, and an old octagonal (eight-sided) wooden schoolhouse.

★ **Historic Charles Town Walking Tour:** Pick up a map at the Jefferson County Museum. Then head out to see more than 30 historic sites within just a few blocks. They include the homes of early residents and the site where John Brown was tried and executed.

Harpers Ferry

★ **Harpers Ferry National Historical Park:** Throughout the park, you'll find museums, hiking trails, battle-fields, and living-history exhibits. Be sure to stop by the restored dry-goods store to see how much candy cost in 1859!

Shepherdstown

★ **Historic Shepherdstown Museum:** This museum displays historical artifacts of the state's first town. It also houses the James Rumsey Steamboat Museum where you'll see a half-size replica of the first steamboat.

MOUNTAINS AND LAKES

THINGS TO DO: Try a pepperoni roll, visit Stonewall Jackson's boyhood home, or learn how miners worked in the 1800s.

Morgantown

★ **Morgantown Glass Museum:** Here you'll see more than 5,000 glass pieces from the 1890s to the 1980s. They were made in the glass factories that once existed in the Morgantown area.

Harpers Ferry National Historical Park

★ **Royce J. & Caroline B. Watts Museum:** This museum preserves the cultural and technological history of the coal, oil, and natural gas industries. Exhibits include miners' lamps, birdcages, fossils, blasting tins and caps, and working models of oil derricks and coal-mining equipment.

★ **John Henry Museum:** Here you'll find exhibits on the beloved folk hero John Henry. There are also displays about African American life and culture in Appalachia.

Fairmont

★ **Country Club Bakery:** Fairmont is the home of pepperoni rolls, and the owner of this bakery is said to have invented them. Try some hot, freshly baked rolls and see why residents are so proud of them.

Grafton

★ **International Mother's Day Shrine:** This 1873 building used to be Andrews Methodist Episcopal Church. On May 10, 1908, the first Mother's Day was observed here. Local resident Anna Jarvis was the force behind creating the national holiday in honor of her own mother.

Weston

★ **Jackson's Mill Historic Area:** This farm is the boyhood home of Civil War general Thomas J. "Stonewall" Jackson. The Jackson family's old mill is now a museum, but the nearby water-powered Blaker's Mill is still operating. You'll see several log cabins and a general store, too.

Jackson's Mill Historic Area

NORTHERN PANHANDLE AND OHIO VALLEY

THINGS TO DO: Check out thousands of toys from the 1800s, ride a train through a zoo, visit the birthplace of West Virginia's statehood, and see a prehistoric Native American mound.

Wheeling

★ **West Virginia Independence Hall:** This is where the Wheeling Convention was held in 1861. During that meeting, 32 counties voted to break away from Virginia and join the Union, leading to West Virginia's statehood. Exhibits explore West Virginia's statehood process and how it fit in with the Civil War.

Kruger Street Toy and Train Museum

★ **Good Zoo & Benedum Theater:** More than 80 species of animals roam this 30-acre (12 ha) zoo, including red wolves, ostriches, and llamas. Inside is a South American rain forest exhibit and the Discovery Lab, where you'll learn about various animals and their habits. If you like, you can ride a train throughout the zoo.

★ **Oglebay Institute Glass Museum:** You'll see more than 3,000 glass objects made in Wheeling's glass factories from 1829 to 1939. A highlight is the Sweeney Punch Bowl, the largest piece of cut lead crystal ever made, at 5 feet (1.5 m) tall and 225 pounds (102 kg).

★ **Schrader Environmental Education Center:** This nature center includes an environment awareness area for children, bird observation points, and many other nature-related exhibits. The EarthTrek Exhibit Hall explores Earth's history and its variety of life-forms. Visitors can also take the Woodland Walkway, a nature trail with signs explaining the area's plants and animals.

★ **Kruger Street Toy and Train Museum:** This museum, in a restored 1800s schoolhouse, displays thousands of toys, including dolls and dollhouses, toy soldiers, trucks and cars, trains, airplanes, ships, space toys, and more. It's full of interactive exhibits, as well as operating model trains.

★ **Palace of Gold:** This stupendous palace rises among the mountaintops in a community called New Vrindaban, named after the town of Vrindaban in India. It was built as a spiritual center in the 1970s by a Hindu religious group called the International Society for Krishna Consciousness. You can tour 10 of the rooms, which are lavishly decorated with stained glass, inlaid marble, and gold leaf. On the grounds are more than 100 fountains and lakes.

Moundsville

★ **Grave Creek Mound:** This is believed to be the largest cone-shaped mound ever made by Native American Mound Builders. People of the Adena culture built it between 250 and 150 BCE, using about 60,000 tons of soil. Exhibits in the nearby museum explain the artifacts and lifestyle of the Adena people.

Parkersburg

★ **Oil and Gas Museum:** Learn about the history of the oil and gas industry in West Virginia through videos, photos, equipment, and interactive displays. You'll see how these industries affected local culture and played a part in the Civil War and West Virginia's statehood.

Palace of Gold

★ **Blennerhassett Mansion:** Located on Blennerhassett Island, this is the reconstructed 1798 mansion of the wealthy Irish immigrant Harman Blennerhassett. Here you can watch a video about his life, tour the mansion, and see three floors of archaeological and historical exhibits. Outdoors, enjoy a horse-drawn wagon ride around the island.

Harrisville

★ **Berdine's Five and Dime:** What can you buy for a nickel or a dime? Back in the early 1900s, you could buy a lot, and you might have shopped at a five-and-dime store. This one, opened in 1908, is the oldest five-and-dime store in the country that's still operating. You can buy candy, tin toys, and many unusual items, though the prices are a bit higher now!

WRITING PROJECTS

Check out these ideas for creating a campaign brochure and writing you-are-there narratives. Or research famous people from West Virginia.

118

ART PROJECTS

You can illustrate the state song, create a dazzling PowerPoint presentation, or learn about the state quarter and design your own.

119

TIMELINE

What happened when? This timeline highlights important events in the state's history—and shows what was happening throughout the United States at the same time.

122

FAST FACTS

Use this section to find fascinating facts about state symbols, land area and population statistics, weather, sports teams, and much more.

126

GLOSSARY

Remember the Words to Know from the chapters in this book? They're all collected here.

125

SCIENCE, TECHNOLOGY, ENGINEERING, & MATH PROJECTS

120

Make weather maps, graph population statistics, and research endangered species that live in the state.

PRIMARY VS. SECONDARY SOURCES

121

So what are primary and secondary sources? And what's the diff? This section explains all that and where you can find them.

BIOGRAPHICAL DICTIONARY

133

This at-a-glance guide highlights some of the state's most important and influential people. Visit this section and read about their contributions to the state, the country, and the world.

RESOURCES

Books and much more. Take a look at these additional sources for information about the state.

138

WRITING PROJECTS

Write a Memoir, Journal, or Editorial for Your School Newspaper!

Picture Yourself . . .

★ In an Adena village. What would your responsibilities be for your family and for the village? Would you tend to the farm and the surrounding agriculture, or would you join your father and the elder men on the hunt?

   SEE: Chapter Two, pages 24–26.

★ Working in a coal mine in the early 20th century. What is life like for coal miners and their families? What dangers would you face?

   SEE: Chapter Four, pages 50–52.

Create an Election Brochure or Web Site!

Run for office! Throughout this book, you've read about some of the issues that concern West Virginia today. As a candidate for governor of West Virginia, create a campaign brochure or Web site.

★ Explain how you meet the qualifications to be governor of West Virginia.

★ Talk about the three or four major issues you'll focus on if you're elected.

★ Remember, you'll be responsible for West Virginia's budget. How would you spend the taxpayers' money?

   SEE: Chapter Seven, pages 86–87.

Create an interview script with a famous person from West Virginia!

★ Research various West Virginians, such as Booker T. Washington, Mother Jones, Betsy Byars, Jerry West, and many more.

★ Based on your research, pick one person you would most like to talk with.

★ Write a script of the interview. What questions would you ask? How would this person answer? Create a question-and-answer format. You may want to supplement this writing project with a voice-recording dramatization of the interview.

   SEE: Chapters Four and Six, pages 52, 77, 78, and 80, and the Biographical Dictionary, pages 133–137.

ART PROJECTS

Create a PowerPoint Presentation or Visitors' Guide

Welcome to West Virginia!

West Virginia's a great place to visit and to live! From its natural beauty to its historic sites, there's plenty to see and do. In your PowerPoint presentation or brochure, highlight 10 to 15 of West Virginia's fascinating landmarks. Be sure to include:

★ a map of the state showing where these sites are located

★ photos, illustrations, Web links, natural history facts, geographic stats, climate and weather, plants and wildlife, and recent discoveries

SEE: Chapter Nine, pages 104–115, and Fast Facts, pages 126–127.

Illustrate the Lyrics to the West Virginia State Song

("The West Virginia Hills")

Use markers, paints, photos, collages, colored pencils, or computer graphics to illustrate the lyrics to "The West Virginia Hills." Turn your illustrations into a picture book, or scan them into PowerPoint and add music.

SEE: The lyrics to "The West Virginia Hills" on page 128.

Research West Virginia's State Quarter

From 1999 to 2008, the U.S. Mint introduced new quarters commemorating each of the 50 states in the order that they were admitted to the Union. Each state's quarter features a unique design on its reverse, or back.

★ Research the significance of the image. Who designed the quarter? Who chose the final design?

★ Design your own West Virginia quarter. What images would you choose for the reverse?

★ Make a poster showing the West Virginia quarter and label each image.

GO TO: www.factsfornow.scholastic.com. Enter the keywords **West Virginia** and look for the link to the West Virginia quarter.

SCIENCE, TECHNOLOGY, ENGINEERING, & MATH PROJECTS

Graph Population Statistics!

★ Compare population statistics (such as ethnic background, birth, death, and literacy rates) in West Virginia counties or major cities.

★ In your graph or chart, look at population density and write sentences describing what the population statistics show; graph one set of population statistics and write a paragraph explaining what the graphs reveal.

SEE: Chapter Six, pages 66–70.

Create a Weather Map of West Virginia!

Use your knowledge of West Virginia geography to research and identify conditions that result in specific weather events. What is it about the geography of West Virginia that makes it vulnerable to floods? Create a weather map or poster that shows the weather patterns over the state. Include a caption explaining the technology used to measure weather phenomenon, and provide data.

SEE: Chapter One, pages 15–16.

Eastern cougar

Track Endangered Species

Using your knowledge of West Virginia's wildlife, research which animals and plants are endangered or threatened.

★ Find out what the state is doing to protect these species.

★ Chart known populations of the animals and plants, and report on changes in certain geographic areas.

SEE: Chapter One, page 20.

PRIMARY VS. SECONDARY SOURCES

What's the Diff?

Your teacher may require at least one or two primary sources and one or two secondary sources for your assignment. So, what's the difference between the two?

★ **Primary sources are original.** You are reading the actual words of someone's diary, journal, letter, autobiography, or interview. Primary sources can also be photographs, maps, prints, cartoons, news/film footage, posters, first-person newspaper articles, drawings, musical scores, and recordings. By the way, when you conduct a survey, interview someone, shoot a video, or take photographs to include in a project, you are creating primary sources!

★ **Secondary sources are what you find in encyclopedias, textbooks, articles, biographies, and almanacs.** These are written by a person or group of people who tell about something that happened to someone else. Secondary sources also recount what another person said or did. This book is an example of a secondary source.

Now that you know what primary sources are—where can you find them?

★ **Your school or local library:** Check the library catalog for collections of original writings, government documents, musical scores, and so on. Some of this material may be stored on microfilm.

★ **Historical societies:** These organizations keep historical documents, photographs, and other materials. Staff members can help you find what you are looking for. History museums are also great places to see primary sources firsthand.

★ **The Internet:** There are lots of sites that have primary sources you can download and use in a project or assignment.

TIMELINE

★ ★ ★

U.S. Events

West Virginia Events

11,000 BCE

c. 10,500 BCE
People first enter what is now West Virginia.

7000 BCE

c. 7000 BCE
Large game animals die out, and people adapt by hunting smaller game.

1000 BCE

c. 1000 BCE
People begin settling in small villages and building burial mounds.

100 BCE

c. 250–150 BCE
Adena people build Grave Creek burial mound.

1000 CE

c. 1000 CE
People of the Fort Ancient culture begin building large towns in what is now western West Virginia.

1400

1492
Christopher Columbus and his crew sight land in the Caribbean Sea.

1600

1607
The first permanent English settlement in North America is established at Jamestown.

c. 1650
People of the Iroquois Confederacy drive other Native groups out of West Virginia.

1671
Thomas Batts and Robert Fallam may be the first Europeans to reach what is now West Virginia.

1700

1727
New Mecklenburg is established as West Virginia's first white settlement.

1768
The Iroquois and Cherokee people are forced to give up their land between the Allegheny Mountains and the Ohio River.

Grave Creek Mound

Iroquois hunter

U.S. Events

West Virginia Events

1774

The Virginia militia defeats Native groups in Lord Dunmore's War.

1775

Western colonists ask to establish their own colony, to be called Westsylvania.

1776

Thirteen American colonies declare their independence from Great Britain.

1787

The U.S. Constitution is written.

1788

Virginia—including today's West Virginia—becomes the 10th U.S. state.

1797

Elisha Brooks builds a salt furnace, beginning the Kanawha Valley's salt industry.

1800

John Brown

1803

The Louisiana Purchase almost doubles the size of the United States.

1859

Abolitionist John Brown leads a raid at Harpers Ferry.

1861-65

The American Civil War is fought between the Northern Union and the Southern Confederacy; it ends with the surrender of the Confederate army, led by General Robert E. Lee.

1861

Virginia secedes from the Union; western counties refuse to secede.

1863

President Abraham Lincoln frees all slaves in the Southern Confederacy with the Emancipation Proclamation.

1863

West Virginia enters the Union as the 35th state.

1872

West Virginia gives African American men the right to vote.

1900

1907

An explosion in the Monongah Mine kills 361 miners.

1912

Bloody conflicts break out between miners and mine owners.

124

U.S. Events

1917-18
The United States engages in World War I.

1929
The stock market crashes, plunging the United States more deeply into the Great Depression.

1941-45
The United States engages in World War II.

1950-53
The United States engages in the Korean War.

1964-73
The United States engages in the Vietnam War.

1991
The United States and other nations engage in the brief Persian Gulf War against Iraq.

2001
Terrorists hijack four U.S. aircraft and crash them into the World Trade Center in New York City, the Pentagon in Arlington, Virginia, and a Pennsylvania field, killing thousands.

2003
The United States and coalition forces invade Iraq.

2008
The United States elects its first African American president, Barack Obama.

West Virginia Events

1921
Mine owners and coal miners battle at Blair Mountain.

Coal mining union

1950s
Eighty thousand coal miners lose their jobs.

1958
People begin holding protests demanding that businesses serve African Americans.

1962
The world's largest movable radio telescope begins operating at the Green Bank observatory.

1968
An explosion in a Farmington coal mine kills 78 people, leading to improved safety regulations.

1990s
Many high-technology companies begin operating in West Virginia.

mid-1990s
Mining companies begin using mountaintop removal to extract coal.

2000

2010
Twenty-nine miners die in an explosion at the Upper Big Branch Mine.

GLOSSARY

abolitionists people who were opposed to slavery and worked to end it

alliance an association among groups that benefits all the members

archaeologists people who study the remains of past human cultures

arsenal a place where weapons are made or stored

brine water saturated with salt

bunker a military defense fortification, usually located underground

civil rights basic human rights that all citizens in a society are entitled to, such as the right to vote

confederacy a group that is formed for a common purpose

continental divide an area of raised terrain that forms a border between two watersheds on a continent

effigy a model; usually a large, clothed dummy that is filled with stuffing

militia a group of citizens organized for military service, as opposed to a regular army

panhandle a narrow strip of land that juts out from a broader area

petition a request for some action, signed by a list of voters

plateau a flat, elevated part of the earth with steep slopes

precipitation all water that falls to the earth, including rain, sleet, hail, snow, dew, fog, or mist

Scots-Irish an ethnic group consisting mainly of Protestant people from Scotland who began settling in northern Ireland in the 1600s

segregated separated from others according to race, class, ethnic group, religion, or other factors

tributary a river that flows into a larger river

FAST FACTS

★ ★ ★

State Symbols

Statehood date June 20, 1863, the 35th state
Origin of state name Virginia was named in honor of England's Queen Elizabeth, the Virgin Queen, and became West Virginia when western counties of Virginia refused to secede during the Civil War.
State capital Charleston
State nickname Mountain State, Panhandle State
State motto *Montani Semper Liberi* ("Mountaineers Are Always Free")
State bird Cardinal
State flower Rhododendron
State fish Brook trout
State animal Black bear
State songs "The West Virginia Hills," "West Virginia, My Home Sweet Home," and "This Is My West Virginia"
State tree Sugar maple
State fair During late August at Lewisburg

State seal

Geography

Total area; rank 24,230 square miles (62,755 sq km); 41st
Land; rank 24,038 square miles (62,258 sq km); 41st
Water; rank 192 square miles (497 sq km); 50th
Inland water; rank 192 square miles (497 sq km); 46th
Geographic center Braxton, 4 miles (6 km) east of Sutton
Latitude 37°10' N to 40°40' N
Longitude 77°40' W to 82°40' W
Highest point Spruce Knob, 4,863 feet (1,482 m)
Lowest point Potomac River, 240 feet (73 m)
Largest city Charleston
Number of counties 55
Longest river Ohio River

Population

Population; rank (2010 census)	1,852,994; 38th
Density (2010 census)	77 persons per square mile (30 per sq km)
Population distribution (2010 census)	49% urban, 51% rural
Ethnic distribution (2010 census)	White persons: 93.2%
	Black persons: 3.4%
	Persons reporting two or more races: 1.3%
	Persons of Hispanic or Latino origin: 1.2%
	Asian persons: 0.7%
	American Indian and Alaska Native persons: 0.2%
	Persons of some other race: 0.1%

Weather

Record high temperature	112°F (44°C) at Martinsburg on July 10, 1936
Record low temperature	−37°F (−38°C) at Lewisburg on December 30, 1917
Average July temperature, Charleston	75°F (24°C)
Average January temperature, Charleston	34°F (1°C)
Average yearly precipitation, Charleston	44 inches (112 cm)

State flag

STATE SONG

★ ★ ★

"The West Virginia Hills"

West Virginia has three state songs. "The West Virginia Hills" (words by Ellen King and music by H. E. Engle) was written in 1885 and adopted in 1961. "West Virginia, My Home Sweet Home" (by Julian G. Hearne Jr.) was written and adopted in 1947. "This Is My West Virginia" (by Iris Bell) was written and adopted in 1962. In 1963, the state legislature declared that all three songs were official and equal, but "The West Virginia Hills" is sung most frequently.

Oh, the West Virginia hills!
How majestic and how grand,
With their summits bathed in glory,
Like our Prince Immanuel's land!
Is it any wonder then,
That my heart with rapture thrills,
As I stand once more with loved ones
On those West Virginia hills?

Oh the hills,
Beautiful hills.
How I love the West Virginia hills!
If o'er sea or land I roam
Still I'll think of happy home,
And the friends among the West Virginia hills.

NATURAL AREAS AND HISTORIC SITES

National Recreation Area

West Virginia's *Gauley River National Recreation Area* features waterways that pass through scenic gorges and valleys and that contain some of the most adventurous white-water rapids in the eastern United States.

National Scenic Trail

A 4-mile (6 km) stretch of the 2,174-mile (3,499 km) *Appalachian National Scenic Trail* passes through the Appalachian Mountains across West Virginia.

National River

West Virginia's *New River Gorge National River* is one of the oldest rivers on the continent and is popular for hiking, camping, and rafting.

National Scenic River

West Virginia has one national scenic river, the *Bluestone National Scenic River*, which is great for kayaking or fishing.

National Historical Parks

The *Chesapeake and Ohio Canal National Historical Park* is the site of the Chesapeake and Ohio Canal, which provided transportation for merchants and ships during the Canal Era.

Harpers Ferry National Historical Park is home to an abolitionist uprising, a Civil War battle, an armory and arsenal, and the confluence of the Potomac and Shenandoah rivers.

National Forests

West Virginia's national forests include *Monongahela National Forest*, located along the eastern border of West Virginia; *George Washington National Forest*, which is shared with Virginia and contains part of the Appalachian Trail; and *Jefferson National Forest*, which is located mostly in Virginia, but a small portion of the forest is in Monroe County, West Virginia.

Spruce Knob-Seneca Rocks National Recreation Area, which is located within Monongahela National Forest and managed by the U.S. Forest Service, has craggy peaks popular with rock climbers.

State Parks

West Virginia's state park system features and maintains dozens of state parks and recreation areas, including *Berkeley Springs State Park* in Morgan County and *Valley Falls State Park* in Marion County.

SPORTS TEAMS

★ ★ ★

NCAA Teams (Division I)

Marshall University *Thundering Herd*
West Virginia University *Mountaineers*

A West Virginia University Mountaineer in action

CULTURAL INSTITUTIONS

Libraries

The *Craft Memorial Library* (Bluefield) houses the Eastern Regional Coal Archives.

The *West Virginia State Library* (Charleston) contains a major collection on the state's history.

Museums

The *Beckley Exhibition Coal Mine* has exhibits of artifacts and photographs showing the history of the local industry.

The *Science Center of West Virginia* (Bluefield) is the first museum in the state to feature hands-on exhibits and programs on electricity and magnetism, light, optics, paleontology, and computer technology.

The *South Charleston Museum* contains, among other artifacts, a section of a 600-year-old giant sycamore.

The *West Virginia & Regional History Center at West Virginia University* (Morgantown) contains one of the largest Appalachian collections in the country.

The *John Brown Wax Museum* (Harpers Ferry) has various exhibits about the man and his raid on the U.S. arsenal.

The *Huntington Museum of Art* is the state's largest fine art museum.

Delf Norona Museum (Moundsville) contains a unique collection of archaeological relics from an American Indian burial mound.

The *Oil and Gas Museum* (Parkersburg) exhibits engines, equipment, and tools used in the early days of the oil and gas business.

Performing Arts

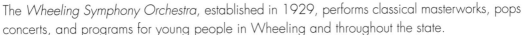

The *Wheeling Symphony Orchestra*, established in 1929, performs classical masterworks, pops concerts, and programs for young people in Wheeling and throughout the state.

The *West Virginia Symphony Orchestra* (Charleston) presents more than 50 concerts throughout the state each year, including classical works and pops series.

Universities and Colleges

In 2011, West Virginia had 13 public and 13 private institutions of higher learning.

ANNUAL EVENTS

January–March

Fasnacht in Helvetia (February)

Leaf Peepers Festival in Davis (March)

April–June

House and Garden Tour in Martinsburg (April)

India Heritage Fair in Charleston (April)

Strawberry Festival in Buckhannon (May)

Vandalia Gathering in Charleston (May)

Webster County Woodchopping Festival in Webster Springs (May)

Wildflower Pilgrimage at Blackwater Falls State Park (May)

First Civil War Land Battle Reenactment in Philippi (June)

West Virginia State Folk Festival in Glenville (June)

Music in the Mountains Bluegrass Festival in Summersville (June)

July–September

Mountain State Art and Craft Fair in Ripley (July)

Fort New Salem Dulcimer Weekend in Salem (August)

Augusta Heritage Festival in Elkins (August)

Appalachian Arts and Crafts Festival in Beckley (late August)

Cherry River Festival in Richwood (August)

Italian Heritage Festival in Clarksburg (August)

West Virginia State Fair in Lewisburg (August)

Hardy County Heritage Weekend in Moorefield (September)

Helvetia Community Fair (September)

Preston County Buckwheat Festival in Kingwood (September)

RoadKill Cook-off and Festival in Marlinton (September)

West Virginia Oil and Gas Festival in Sistersville (September)

October–December

Black Walnut Festival in Spencer (October)

Mountain State Forest Festival in Elkins (October)

New River Gorge Bridge Day Festival in Fayetteville (October)

Winter Festival of Lights in Wheeling (early November–early January)

Eighteenth-Century Christmas Market at Pricketts Fort in Fremont (November and December)

Allen Appel (1945–) is an author whose time-travel novels include *Time After Time, Twice upon a Time,* and *Till the End of Time.* He grew up in Parkersburg and graduated from West Virginia University.

"Mad Anne" Bailey (1742–1825) was a frontierswoman and scout who lived in what is now Charleston. During Indian wars in 1791, she rode 100 miles (161 km) through the wilderness to get ammunition for Fort Lee.

Sandra Belton (1939–) is a children's book author who bases many of her stories on her experiences growing up as an African American in Beckley.

Julia Bonds (1952–2011) was an environmental activist known as the godmother of the anti-mountaintop coal removal movement. Born in Marfork Hollow, many members of her family were coal miners.

Daniel Boone (1734–1820) was a pioneer and scout who blazed the Wilderness Road through the Cumberland Gap. In the 1790s, he lived in Clendenin's Settlement, which became today's Charleston. He also served in Virginia's assembly.

Belle Boyd (1843–1900), born in Martinsburg, was a Confederate spy during the Civil War. She often provided valuable information to fellow West Virginian General Thomas "Stonewall" Jackson.

George Brett

George Brett (1953–) is a former baseball player with the Kansas City Royals. He was born in Glen Dale.

Maurice Brooks See page 20.

John Brown See page 44.

Betsy Byars See page 78.

Robert Byrd See page 88.

Alexander Campbell (1788–1866) was a minister who cofounded the Disciples of Christ church. He founded Bethany College in 1840.

Stephen Coonts (1946–) is a best-selling writer of suspense novels who is best known as the creator of the Jake Grafton series of adventure-thrillers. He was born in the tiny mining town of Buckhannon.

John Corbett

Jennifer Garner

John Corbett (1961–) is an actor who appeared in the TV series *Northern Exposure* and *The Visitor* and the movie *My Big Fat Greek Wedding*. He was born in Wheeling.

Cornstalk See page 36.

George Crumb (1929–) is a composer known for using unusual sound effects in his music. He won the 1968 Pulitzer Prize for music. He was born in Charleston.

Phyllis Curtin (1921–) is a soprano opera singer. She was born in Clarksburg.

Martin Delany (1812–1885) was a journalist and activist who served in the Union army. He was born a free black in Charleston.

Bob Denver (1935–2005) was an actor who starred in the TV series *Gilligan's Island*. He lived for a time in Princeton.

Hazel Dickens (1935–2011) was a bluegrass singer and musician who advocated for the rights of coal miners and working people in her music. A native of Montcalm in Mercer County, she was born to a mining family.

Joanne Dru (1922–1996) was an actor, born in Logan, who starred with John Wayne in *Red River* and *She Wore a Yellow Ribbon*.

Jennifer Garner (1972–) is an actor who received the 2002 Golden Globe and several Emmy Award nominations for her role as Sydney Bristow in the TV spy drama *Alias*. She was raised in Princeton and Charleston.

Henry Louis Gates Jr. See page 58.

Homer Hickam (1943–) is an author whose novel *Rocket Boys: A Memoir* is based on his childhood in Coalwood. It was made into the 1999 movie *October Sky*.

Martin Delany

Don Knotts

Robert Lee "Sam" Huff (1934–) is a former star linebacker for the New York Giants and Washington Redskins football teams. He was born in Edna Gas.

Thomas "Stonewall" Jackson See page 47.

Anna Jarvis (1864–1948), a native of Webster, was the creator of Mother's Day, which was recognized as a national holiday in 1914.

Johnnie Johnson (1924–2005) was a pianist and blues musician best known for his work with rock and roll pioneer Chuck Berry. Born in Fairmont, Johnson was inducted into the Rock and Roll Hall of Fame in 2001.

Mary Harris "Mother" Jones See page 52.

Lawrence Kasdan (1949–), raised in Morgantown, is a filmmaker. He wrote *Raiders of the Lost Ark* and co-wrote several Star Wars movies.

John S. Knight (1894–1981) was a journalist and publisher who developed the Knight-Ridder newspaper chain. He won the 1968 Pulitzer Prize for editorial writing. He was born in Bluefield.

Don Knotts (1924–2006) was an actor best known for playing Barney Fife in the television series *The Andy Griffith Show*. He was born in Morgantown.

John Knowles (1926–2001) was an author best known for his novel *A Separate Peace*. He was born in Fairmont.

Ben Mahmoud (1935–2009) was a modern artist whose works have been exhibited throughout the United States and other countries. He was born and raised in Charleston.

Christy Martin (1968–) is a female boxer nicknamed the Coal Miner's Daughter. She was born in Bluefield and grew up in Mullens.

Kathy Mattea (1959–) is a country music singer. She was born in South Charleston and grew up in Cross Lanes.

Bill Mazeroski (1936–) played second base for the Pittsburgh Pirates and won eight Gold Glove Awards for his outstanding fielding skills. Yet he is best remembered for hitting the game-winning home run in the seventh game of the 1960 World Series. Born in Wheeling, "Maz" was inducted into the Baseball Hall of Fame in 2001.

Kathy Mattea

Jon McBride (1943–), a native of Charleston, is a former astronaut who served as the pilot on the space shuttle *Challenger* in 1984. After retiring from NASA in 1989, he ran a business and was president of a workers' union in his home state.

Charlie McCoy (1941–) is a singer and musician who has recorded with such famous performers as Johnny Cash, Bob Dylan, and Elvis Presley. A native of Oak Hill, he was the musical director of the popular TV show *Hee Haw* for 19 years.

Louise McNeill (1911–1993) was a poet and a historian of Appalachia who was West Virginia's poet laureate from 1979 until her death. She was born in Buckeye.

Morgan Morgan (1688–1766) was an early settler from Wales. His son Zackquill founded Morgantown.

Walter Dean Myers See page 79.

John Forbes Nash (1928–) is a mathematician who won the Nobel Prize in Economics in 1994. His life was portrayed in the movie *A Beautiful Mind*. He was born in Bluefield.

Brad Paisley

Brad Paisley (1972–) is a country music singer and songwriter. He was born in Glen Dale.

Francis Harrison Pierpont (1814–1899) was governor of the Reorganized State of Virginia and pushed for the creation of a separate state. He is called the Father of West Virginia. He was born near Morgantown.

Mary Lou Retton See page 81.

Walter Reuther (1907–1970) was one of the most influential labor leaders of the 20th century. He was president of the United Automobile Workers (UAW) and the Congress of Industrial Organizations (CIO). He was born in Wheeling.

Cecil Roberts Jr. See page 60.

John D. "Jay" Rockefeller IV See page 89.

Walter E. "Jack" Rollins (1906–1973) was a songwriter who co-wrote "Frosty the Snowman" and "Here Comes Peter Cottontail." He was born in Keyser.

Walter Reuther

Cynthia Rylant (1954–) is the author of more than 100 books for children and young adults. She grew up in Cool Ridge and Beaver, and most of her books are about life in the Appalachian region.

Harry Sinclair (1876–1956), born in Benwood, was the founder of Sinclair Oil, one of the largest oil companies in the United States.

Beau Smith (1954–), a native of Huntington, is a comic book writer best known for his work at Eclipse Comics, Image Comics, and DC Comics.

E. M. Statler See page 97.

Eleanor Steber (1914–1990) was a soprano opera singer and concert star. She was born in Wheeling.

Cyrus Vance (1917–2002) was the U.S. secretary of state from 1977 to 1980. He was born in Clarksburg.

Booker T. Washington See page 77.

Harold Tucker Webster (1885–1952) was a cartoonist who created *The Timid Soul* cartoon panel, with its wimpy character Caspar Milquetoast. He was born in Parkersburg.

Jerry West (1938–) is a basketball Hall of Famer who played for the Los Angeles Lakers. He was the first player to score more than 4,000 points in the play-offs. He was born in Chelyan.

Bill Withers

Bill Withers (1938–) is a singer and songwriter best known for songs such as "Ain't No Sunshine" and "Lovely Day." He was born in Slab Fork.

Carter G. Woodson See page 49.

Chuck Yeager (1923–) is a former U.S. Air Force test pilot. In 1947, he became the first pilot to fly faster than the speed of sound. He was born in Myra.

Steve Yeager (1948–) is a former baseball player for the Los Angeles Dodgers and the Seattle Mariners. He was born in Huntington.

Chuck Yeager

RESOURCES

★　★　★

BOOKS

Nonfiction

Crompton, Samuel Willard. *The Raid on Harpers Ferry: John Brown's Rebellion*. New York: Chelsea House, 2010.

Dolbear, Emily J., and Peter Benoit. *The Iroquois*. New York: Children's Press, 2011.

Gregory, Josh. *The Revolutionary War*. New York: Children's Press, 2011.

Santella, Andrew. *The French and Indian War*. New York: Children's Press, 2012.

Whiting, Jim. *Booker T. Washington*. Broomall, PA: Mason Crest Publishers, 2010.

Fiction

Belton, Sandra. *McKendree*. New York: Greenwillow Books, 2000.

Byars, Betsy. *The Summer of the Swans*. New York: Puffin Books, 2004.

Hickam, Homer. *Rocket Boys: A Memoir*. New York: Delacorte Press, 1998.

Rylant, Cynthia. *Missing May*. New York: Orchard Books, 1992.

Seabrooke, Brenda. *The Haunting of Swain's Fancy*. New York: Dutton Juvenile, 2003.

FACTS FOR NOW

Visit this Scholastic Web site for more information on West Virginia:
www.factsfornow.scholastic.com
Enter the keywords **West Virginia**

INDEX

★ ★ ★

AUTHOR'S TIPS AND SOURCE NOTES

★   ★   ★

West Virginia was an exciting state to research because its people have such interesting backgrounds and traditions. *West Virginia: A History* by John Alexander Williams provided invaluable insights into the events that shaped West Virginia. A book by Otis K. Rice and Stephen W. Brown, also titled *West Virginia: A History*, provided detailed information on prehistoric peoples and early explorations in West Virginia. Another interesting source was *The German Element in the United States* by Albert Bernhardt Faust, published in 1909. It gave me a good picture of how German settlers first moved into the Valley of Virginia, as the Shenandoah Valley was called.